IDIOT

IDIOT

LIFE STORIES FROM
THE CREATOR OF
HELP HELEN SMASH

LAURA CLERY

G

GALLERY BOOKS

NEW YORK   LONDON   TORONTO   SYDNEY   NEW DELHI

G

Gallery Books
An Imprint of Simon & Schuster, Inc.
1230 Avenue of the Americas
New York, NY 10020

Many names and identifying details have been changed.

First Gallery Books hardcover edition September 2019

GALLERY BOOKS and colophon are registered trademarks of Simon & Schuster, Inc.

For information about special discounts for bulk purchases, please contact Simon & Schuster Special Sales at 1-866-506-1949 or business@simonandschuster.com.

The Simon & Schuster Speakers Bureau can bring authors to your live event. For more information or to book an event, contact the Simon & Schuster Speakers Bureau at 1-866-248-3049 or visit our website at www.simonspeakers.com.

Interior design by Alexis Minieri

Manufactured in the United States of America

10   9   8

Library of Congress Cataloging-in-Publication Data is available.

ISBN 978-1-9821-0194-7
ISBN 978-1-9821-0196-1 (ebook)

To my momma.
For loving me fully and believing in me always.
I love you.

CONTENTS

CHAPTER 1

Oh, the Places I've Peed

I'm tall—six feet, to be exact. I've always been really tall for my age. Remember when Mary Poppins pulled that long-ass hat stand out of her Magic Bag? That's what it was like when the doctors pulled me out of my mom's vagina. With my full head of hair, I looked like a hat stand wearing a wig. Still do!

By the time I was fourteen, I had outgrown my twin-size bed. So naturally, I started sleeping on the living room couch. Which meant that sleep was soon replaced with infomercial watching. I'd wake up late every morning, my hat stand–body sprawled across the couch, surrounded by Post-its scribbled with 1-800 numbers and names of useless products: the after-party mess from my late-night infomercial benders. When my mom walked into the living room in the morning, I'd leap off the couch and accost her.

"MOM? Mom! We *have* to get the Hawaii Chair. We need it; you don't understand—it's only six easy payments of $19.99. You sit in it and it sways your butt around, and then you have abs in a MONTH. I saw the before and after! It's real! Mom? Come back."

I followed her into the kitchen and sat down on an insufferable regular chair. To give her the full picture, I swayed my hips on the chair. After watching her daughter grind awkwardly for a good five minutes, she said, "Laura, you're just gonna sit on that thing for thirty minutes and then puke." She didn't get me the Hawaii Chair.

She never got me ANYTHING from infomercials. In spite of this deprivation, I did have a pretty happy childhood. I grew up in the most ideal suburb you could ever imagine: Downers Grove, Illinois—a working- / middle-class town twenty minutes outside Chicago.

Now you might be thinking, "Ha-ha! DOWNERS Grove? Is everyone on Xanax all the time?" If we're gonna be realistic, then yeah, probably. Maybe that's why everyone is so nice. It's a chill suburb. All the children play out on the street, and the community is really close. I'm pretty sure we even got on a list of the "Top Ten Places to Raise Kids" in, like, 2006 or something. And almost nothing has changed since then. It's a lovely place where you're born and never leave.

Okay, that sounds more ominous than I mean. You never leave . . . in a good way! You don't leave because it has everything you'd ever need! Take my parents, for example. They were both born a few minutes away in Oak Park, Illinois. They grew up in the same neighborhood and went to the same high school. They had a love story straight from the movie *Grease*. My dad was a greaser, leather jacket and all. He was in a gang—well, a white, middle-class, high school gang. They just stole stuff, vandalized buildings, and smoked weed all the time. My mother, on the other hand, was a total prep. She was on the honor roll, a cheerleader, and had a reserved and sweet disposition. And when they were on opposite sides of town, they would both randomly break into the same song.

Okay, that last detail was a lie, but the rest is completely true.

They met at an April Fool's party. My dad saw my mom from across the room and knew she was the one. He was sixteen and she was fifteen. That's right, a decade and a half out of the womb and he knew she was the one. He asked her out again and again . . . and she repeatedly said no. In her defense, he had a girlfriend at the time.

When recounting the story, my dad jokingly complains, "She made me break up with my girlfriend!" He apparently did not want to. After he did, he and my mom started going out. And that was it. They married and had my eldest sister, Tracy; my middle sister, Colleen; and me, Laura. They settled in a home thirty minutes from the houses they grew up in.

Even though they upheld the local tradition of staying in the Chicagoland area, my parents were a bit of an anomaly in our pristine town. As just one example, in a suburb that embodied practicality, my dad bought my mother a Sebring convertible. This was in a city that has good weather for like . . . two weeks out of the year. Winters in Illinois are brutal and last forever, and my dad bought my mother a car whose main feature was a top that came off and exposed us all to the rain, sleet, and snow.

Soon enough the fabric roof got a hole in it, and now they keep a bucket in the backseat for when it rains. (Yes, twenty years later they still have the car.) But my parents really wanted to enjoy those two weeks of nice weather per year. I love that about them.

Downers Grove is a mostly Catholic town with strong family values. Not so much religious as culturally Catholic. By far, my family had the most . . . um . . . passionate opinions about religion. One of my dad's favorite dinnertime musings was "FUCK ORGANIZED RELIGION! It's bullshit. And eat another hot dog, Laura, you're too skinny!" My family were the only atheists in town. My dad was bent on making sure we knew that church was brainwashing.

No matter what ideals they grew up with, no matter who they were speaking to, my parents were incredibly open-minded. They were authentic. They never pressured me to get married, and they made it very clear that they would love me if I was gay. Even though we were constantly struggling financially, they made sure I never felt the pressure to get a stable nine-to-five job if I didn't want one. I wouldn't trade those two for the world. Well, maybe for the *world*, but nothing less!

While all the other parents in town were encouraging their kids to pursue practical careers, my mom and dad didn't blink twice when I told them at age eleven I was going to be a famous actress. "You can do it, sweetheart. We believe in you!"

My dad would take the liberal parenting a bit further when he would also say things like "When you try acid, make sure you're in a comfortable setting."

"I'm not gonna try acid, Dad."

"Oh come on, Laura, you gotta try acid."

I never did try acid. I guess it was my way of rebelling?

—

In grammar school a few other kids asked me, "When did you make your Holy Communion?"

I had never heard of Holy Communion. I asked them what it was. Then they frowned and said, "You're going to hell."

Nine-year-olds say the darndest things!

That day, I went home and asked my mother, "Why are we going to hell?" She was a bit alarmed. I even insisted she teach me a prayer so that I would fit in with the other kids. But even when I tried, I just didn't fit in with them. The small rejections made it hard for me to talk in school. I lacked any confidence once I stepped inside the classroom.

Today, I really appreciate this aspect of how I was raised. In a town where everyone passively accepted religion as one of the defining factors of our community, my parents never forced a religion on me. My dad would say, "When you're old enough to research different religions and make that decision for yourself, I want you to be able to do that." And I did. I've been able to go my own way and find a spirituality that I fully believe in and speaks to me. Hail Satan!

Just kidding.

Aaaand . . . there might have been one other reason why I didn't fit in well. I had a really morbid sense of humor. And no one wants to talk to the skinny, quiet child making creepy death jokes in the corner of the room.

So I channeled it all at home. My favorite thing to do was write and direct horror movies. I'd grab my family's camcorder, all the kids in the neighborhood, and a butter knife (which is obviously a murderer's top weapon of choice). Then I'd record these cheesy short horror movies. It was difficult to be both the villain and the director, but I made it work. Video camera in one hand and butter knife clenched in the other, the frame would show just my tiny, dubiously armed fist and my neighbor John running away, screaming as I chased him.

So . . . you can imagine how popular I was with the church-y kids at school. Have you ever read one of those psychology textbooks where they tell you the traits of the eldest, middle, and youngest sibling? My sisters and I fit exactly. Tracy, the eldest, follows rules, is strict, and did whatever our parents told us to do. Colleen is an introverted oddball who played songs on the guitar written in French and read books for fun. I was the annoying loudmouth comedienne that everyone loved. (Right? Right?) All I ever wanted to do was make people laugh.

When I became painfully shy and quiet at school during those years, it was VERY out of character for me. Luckily, that's when I met Maggie, my childhood soul mate. I was in third grade, and we were in the talent show together. She was singing Karen Carpenter's "Top of the World" at the top of her lungs. I remember she was so loud that her voice became shaky trying to handle it. My mother had been rehearsing my sisters and me in a roughly harmonized rendition of "Chapel of Love" and getting up on that stage absolutely terrified me. I knew how difficult it was to sing in front of people, and because of that, I was SO impressed by Maggie. I remember being enamored by her and thinking she was the bravest, most confident person I had ever seen. And then when she got off the stage, she punched a boy for making fun of her. That's seriously badass.

I approached her, told her I liked her headband, and we were attached at the hip after that. We spent every waking moment with each other—either she slept at my house, or we stayed up on the phone with each other. (I would have stayed at her house too, but we just got away with much more mischief at my house.) With her, I finally came out of my shell. We really were oddballs together. It was finally okay for my strangeness and humor to come out.

I even loved her family. Maggie's mom was a stay-at-home mom who went back to college in her late forties and started working again. Her dad was this slick FBI agent. He was very strict, so different from my own parents. #whatisstructure?

The best part of Maggie's family was her older sister. To the rest of the world, she was a high school theater nerd. To me, she was the most incredible actress I had ever seen. We went to see her high school play once. It was a comedy and she had complete command of the audience. Laughter rang out at one point and I remember thinking to myself, *I want to do what she's doing*. I was eleven years old, and it was the moment I decided I wanted to be an actress.

Being in Maggie's atmosphere made a huge impact on my life. We loved to try to thrill each other. It became kind of a contest as to who could be the most shocking. In school, we would write each other the most fucked up notes we could think of to see who could get a bigger rise out of the other person. We knew some curse words at this point in our lives, but we didn't exactly know how to use them. So we inserted them into sentences where they sounded good! That's how words work, right?

She passed me one that said: "My arm shits smell. It really fucks that we can't go to Six Flags Great America this weekend."

To which I'd respond: "Can you ass me some water?"

We were pretty legit.

In sixth grade, Maggie's note was intercepted by the principal. The principal read the note and then told Maggie, "You need to read this aloud to your parents." We both looked at each other frantically. Her FBI agent dad would NOT be cool about this, to say the least.

"Oh SHIT," we both muttered to each other, finally using the word correctly!

Not only did we both get so much detention, but the next day there was an assembly for just the girls in our school about the importance of being a lady. Our principal had a bold opening line: "When you say 'shit' or 'fuck' or 'bitch' it is very unbecoming, girls." I avoided her eye contact at all costs, while Maggie nodded along, sardonically, an air of fake concern about her. Like I said, Maggie was badass.

Next on Maggie and Laura's list of shocking activities? Public urination. Maggie and I would pee in public all over the place. That's normal, right? She would go outside of a Walmart, I would go on her neighbor's lawn, we both took turns outside of a public library, again and again until we ran out of places. Or until the neighbors started to notice spots of dead grass on their lawns.

But as expected, our game of "Who could pee in the most shocking place?" got old quickly. Fortunately, Maggie knew how to take things up a notch.

In sixth grade, we took a trip to Six Flags Great America and stayed at the Holiday Inn. That night we were in the hot tub, splashing each other while sitting across from an older couple who were just trying to enjoy their vacation.

"Can you ladies stop it, please? You're being disruptive," the woman said.

"Yeah, Laura," Maggie said, "stop being disruptive."

I frowned and shoved her awkwardly, but quieted down. The

woman sighed. I looked down at the bubbling water to avoid the old couple's shaming glaucoma-glare. I saw Maggie roll her eyes.

"Can we go back to the room?" I asked Maggie.

"Nope. I want to get pruney."

I sighed. A moment of silence and then Maggie smiled at me with this devilish grin. I looked at her, confused. "What?" I whispered. And then . . . I felt it. Something soft and mushy in my hand. I lifted my hand out of the water—and screamed!

It was Maggie's shit. She had shit in the Jacuzzi. AND THE SHIT WAS IN MY HAND.

I was so fucking shocked that I threw the shit as hard as I could, hopped out of the Jacuzzi, and jumped into the pool. The lady sitting across from me screamed. I may or may not have gotten some shit on her.

To this day I won't go in a Holiday Inn Jacuzzi. I hope Maggie's not upset with me for sharing that. Maybe I should change her name. Maddie. Identity concealed! Nice, Laura.

Maggie and I were fucking weird and adventurous and I loved it more than anything. We would striptease for each other to "The Sign" by Ace of Base. (Which really is a top striptease song, I'd say, and definitely still holds up.) We'd give each other half naked massages by candlelight and we'd go to Barnes & Noble and find the Victoria Secret catalogs in the back and tape pictures of our faces inside of them. This, in retrospect, was probably highly disturbing for the next person who opened them up. Someone in the market for Victoria Secret probably didn't bet on seeing a smiling eleven-year-old's face taped above some huge tits. But we didn't care!

We very badly wanted to grow up and be women and *know things* about our bodies. We were curious. In Downers Grove, not many people were interested in educating prepubescent girls about sex. So it was just me and Maggie against the world, figuring things out for ourselves. Living in a weird, amazing bubble.

At school, Maggie and I had other friends for a while. But as she and I got more and more drawn into our own world, our other friends became convinced we were lesbians and cut us off from hanging out. I guess they thought lesbian meant . . . weird?

But we didn't care. If they were going to abandon us for being too strange, then I was happy to see them go. Together, it was okay to be different. To be who we were. Maggie became the star of all my horror movies, and fake-stabbing my best friend with a butter knife became my favorite pastime.

Despite living in a comfortable middle-class town, my family never seemed to have any money. We were pretty much always broke. But in spite of all that, I never felt poor. Probably because families hide things well from the youngest child! But also because I felt safe and we always had enough to eat. And if I ever wanted expensive things, I would just steal them. Problem solved!

My parents did a good job of making me feel like money wasn't an issue. They made it a point for us to have experiences that normal families would have, like going on vacation—even if they were vacations at which most people would turn up their noses. Every year my dad's whole side of the family would go to The Golden Horse Ranch in Wisconsin. Every year, you guys. I hear some families, like, try to see different parts of the world eventually? Not us!

This ranch was small and completely broken-down. The cabins would have mice in them, and when we'd ask the front desk for help, they would hand us a cat and say "Figure it out." There were horses and literal barn dances and terrible beige food and tiny cabins that were too hot and always a bit moist.

Which is all to say: it was awesome!

I don't think there's anything better than being out in the wilderness with the people you love, staying out late, climbing around the forest, making the most of your ill-functioning cabin, and running around horses redolent of poop. It was also when I got to try adult things for the first time. It's like when you're on vacation, the rules don't apply.

When I was in junior high, I brought Maggie and a couple friends with me to the ranch. My sister Colleen wanted to get us drunk for the first time. She poured a shot of vodka into each of our cups of SunnyD and we gulped it down, eager to see what it felt like. In the blink of an eye we were wasted.

In our drunken stupor, we thought that the coolest thing we could do would be to climb out the window instead of using the door. Because, you know, falling into scratchy bushes is really cool! So we did that. We stumbled over to the rec center and played drunk bingo. Well, it was technically normal bingo. But for us it was drunk bingo. I'm sure all of the senior citizens were a bit confused by our enthusiasm. Especially after Maggie yelled "BINGO!" for the fourth time.

"I'VE ONLY CALLED THREE NUMBERS; I KNOW YOU DON'T HAVE A BINGO, MISS."

When we walked back to the cabin, each of us now suffering a dehydration headache, my mom was outside. Arms crossed, furious. Or was she . . . scratching her arms? Either way, she looked super mad. *Oh crap, what did we do?* I thought to myself. She just glared and didn't say a word as we passed her. There was a soft buzzing noise. That's weird. As we walked inside . . . it got louder and louder. We looked up to see an ominous black cloud across the ceiling of the cabin.

It wasn't a cloud. It was THOUSANDS AND THOUSANDS OF MOSQUITOS trapped inside our cabin. We had left the window open and the light on and they all came swarming inside. I screamed and tried to run out, but my mom was blocking the doorway. "FIX THIS," she said.

Yikes. Colleen and my friends and I spent the next three hours standing on chairs with shoes on our hands, stomping on the bugs on the ceiling. I'd kill four at a time with my Sketchers, but then the bodies would fall down on my face. Yum!

As someone who struggled with alcoholism years later, I can look back and see that drinking had always brought consequences.

—

As Maggie and I got older, our insular duo got less insular. We joined a group of popular girls called The Twelve, named both because we were twelve years old and there were twelve of us. Creative geniuses over here! We were your typical group of bitchy junior high kids, complete with professional photos taken at the Yorktown mall. Our leader was named Erica (of course) and she was this beautiful, blonde, popular cheerleader, who was dating Tyler, the most popular guy in school. All the boys were in love with her because she had tits from a young age. She's super nice now, but was a total bitch back then. It wasn't her fault, though. Today, none of those girls have a mean bone in their bodies. Something about being that age makes everyone a little mean.

Once we were in this group, all of a sudden everything mattered. How you did your hair, who you dated, what brand of socks you had on. Unfortunately, the best socks my mom could get me were Tommy Hilfangures.

"We said we were wearing *Abercrombie* shirts today, Laura."

I looked down at the logo on my shirt and mumbled back, "This IS Aberzombie."

"What did you say?"

"Nothing."

Even if I didn't have the right clothes, I found my place in our crew as the entertainer. There was one fateful lunch period where I stuck grapes up my nose and Erica proclaimed "Laura is totally, like, the funny one!" From then on I was their clown, and I was good at it.

We all had our place. Erica was the leader; I was the funny one; Holly was the shining light of positivity. She could see a bright side to everything. You got picked last for basketball? Then there's no pressure! You got detention? It's extra time to finish your homework! To this day she is the nicest, most positive woman I know, and one of my best friends. Instead of detention, now she gets excited to go to the DMV because . . . who the fuck knows?

My job as The Entertainer fit me well. I could make these girls laugh their asses off. We would make prank phone calls, or rather I would. All the other girls would have to go in the other room and listen on the muted second line because they'd be in tears, laughing so hard that it would have ruined the prank.

One night, we got tired of pranking the local pizza restaurant. We decided to do something to Tyler, Erica's boyfriend. He lived three doors down from Holly's house, where we were having our sleepover that night. Now, Tyler was like the golden boy of our school. He was so sweet and well liked, he had this charismatic personality and great smile that just won everyone over. And he was also one of our best friends. So we wanted to do something that would REALLY get him.

Here's what we came up with: We put a training bra on his front porch and ran home giggling. Then we called his house. There was no answer, but we left the following voice mail: "Boobs on your porch! Boobs on your porch!" Pretty scandalous, right? But he didn't even call back! Maybe he was out at soccer practice. An hour later, we called again. "Boobs on your porch! Boobs on your porch!" Again nothing. Well, damn.

The sleepover continued as normal and we went home the next day. But when Monday rolled around, I got a call from Holly. It was a conference call with all the girls on it. Holly was freaking out. "There are cops outside Tyler's house! They're onto us; they know we did boobs on the porch! What do we do??"

Fuck fuck fuck. We all panicked! Jail time was definitely imminent. Even Holly couldn't spin this as a positive.

"How many cops??"

"Literally two cop cars!"

"I can't get arrested! Dance team tryouts are next week!"

I tried to be the voice of reason. "Just lay low everybody. Just lay low."

We all stayed indoors that day. That night we got a call. Tyler— our good friend Tyler—had committed suicide that day, in his basement.

None of us knew he was even close to his breaking point. He had always seemed so happy. None of the "typical" signs were there— he wasn't an outcast, he never had trouble socializing. It was the first time we were faced with death that wasn't about our pets or grandparents—it was someone just like us. At that age you think you're immortal and invincible. I think Tyler's death woke us up to the harsh reality that you could be here one day and gone the next. And we had that wake-up call at age twelve.

That night we congregated at Holly's house again. Three doors down from Tyler's. We cried and cried.

After that, The Twelve were a lot more compassionate. A lot quieter. Some of us went our separate ways after junior high, but that grief bonded us in a way nothing else could have. It set the tone for the rest our adolescence: that reality outside of childhood isn't as bright as you want it to be.

I started to feel tired of caring what people thought about me. I didn't want to care. I didn't want people to feel like they had to put on a happy face around me. Or that they had to pretend to be stronger than they felt. What if Tyler had been able to talk to us about how he was feeling? What if we were all able to be more authentic?

I threw away all my Tommy Hilfangure socks and Aberzombie shirts, as well as the sequin scrunchies and everything I had shoplifted in order to fit in with The Twelve. Laura Clery was about to be her goddamn self, bitches.

CHAPTER 2

High School Hammer Time

Maggie and I changed a little after we hit high school. Our ambitions changed. For example, she wanted to give the speech at graduation. And I wanted to do drugs. Call us high achievers, because we BOTH reached our goals!

I don't blame her for wanting to straighten up. I mean, she had straight As. She was good at school. Academic achievement was her ticket to success. But it wasn't for me. I tested terribly, couldn't focus, and I'd ditch class whenever I could. I also took geometry three times, and *not* because I loved it.

Almost failing school was fine, though. So what if I got bad grades? I was going to be an actress. It was my destiny. And you don't need geometry to act, dammit.

I was very disruptive in class. (Kids . . . don't be like me.) I just didn't see the point of school. It was like a horrible spiral where I didn't try because I wasn't doing well and didn't care to do well, and then my teachers would hate me, and then I would be more disruptive because . . . it's not like I had any student-teacher relationships to preserve!

I was not a joy to have in class. For me, class was just a time for me to practice bits on my classmates—try to make everyone laugh. My teachers might have hated it, but to everyone else, I was a riot. I'd do one bit where I'd sit right in the middle of the classroom, where I knew people could see me from every angle. I'd fill up my mouth with water, hold it in there, and then pretend to be asleep. And then I would drool excessively until I heard whispers turn into exclamations of "AWWWW SICK!!!" It was very committed preparation. I took clowning around seriously, you guys.

Then I would fake waking up all startled, and splash everyone nearby. Classmates started trying to avoid my splash zone. But in a huge, overcrowded public school, it was either sit next to me or sit on the floor! When I worked in the speech office, I would photocopy pictures of my ass and pass them out. It was the original unsolicited dick pic.

Because I was very well known for causing a disturbance, this meant Maggie and I had to go our separate ways. With no hard feelings at all—she would still come over to my house in the middle of the night to watch movies with me in secret and sometimes we'd sneak into the porn section of Family Video after class—but beginning my freshman year, I was already starting to be known as a bad kid. I was tainting her image.

Because my parents were liberal hippies, I didn't need to hide my bad-kid tendencies from anyone. I don't think the following is the normal conversation parents have with their kids about weed:

Dad: Laura, are you smoking weed?

Laura: Um . . . I don't know. Why?

Dad: Here's twenty bucks. Can you get me some?

I got away with a lot. I was kind of an odd bad kid, though. I wasn't completely removed from school or in a "bad-kid clique." I was friends with people in all types of cliques and did extracurriculars like student council. But frequently I also happened to ditch class to smoke weed. Life is all about balance, you guys!

Once we took a field trip to downtown Chicago for a student council convention (of course I'm going to do an extracurricular that gets me out of class!). As I stared out the window of the bus, I made mental notes of all the shops I wanted to check out when I inevitably ditched the entire event. As I was exiting the bus and planning my escape, I saw this boy in my grade that I had seen being bullied earlier that day. The twist was that he yelled back at the jocks who were making fun of him, which was badass.

In his black jacket and black jeans, he was the best-dressed bullied nerd I had ever seen. I looked down at my weird sweatpants and touched my topknot, which was currently frizzing out. My mom actually made sweatpants, so I had like ten pairs and it was all I wore. Some might have called it slovenly, but I say: Ahead of my time! Athleisure is in now!!!

I approached him. "Wanna ditch this and smoke a cigarette with me?" I asked.

"I can't. I have a boner for student council."

"You . . . what?"

"I'm joking. Let's get out of here."

We slipped away from the group. I lit a cigarette, handed it to him, and he winced as he took a drag. He was pretending to be chill about it, but I later found out that this was his first cigarette! He just jumped at the opportunity to hang out with me because I was apparently a "cool kid" in my homemade sweatpants.

From then on, we were attached at the hip. We'd do everything together. I would defend him a lot from the guys who picked on him, but I don't think he truly even needed me. Jack had this incredible "fuck you" sort of attitude. He didn't care what people thought about him. He just was who he was. He didn't come out as gay to me until years later (because of course it takes a long time to build up that courage), but he was always authentically himself. Always. I loved and admired that about him.

Every day we would smoke weed and ditch school. After we had too many unexcused absences, I had the brilliant idea of getting us actual excused absences. I always had a knack for accents and voices . . . and I had his mom's voice down pat. I'd call the front desk of our school: "Hi, this is Caroline McCalpin calling. I need to come pick up Jack, so please let his teachers know, thanks."

It worked every time. Other kids started to notice and ask me for my services.

"Can you call me out of school too?"

"Yes. That will be twenty-five dollars."

I'd press *67 to make my number private, so the school had no way of seeing that everyone's mom had the same phone number. It was foolproof, you guys. I got pretty sophisticated with my mom voices, too. I could do a Macedonian mom, an Irish mom, a New Jersey mom . . . Jenna's, Lisa's, and Jeff's mothers respectively. I could do whatever anyone wanted from me. I once excused a kid for an entire week.

I started getting cocky about my ability . . . I probably crossed a line when I began making calls to the office *while* I was in class. In my defense, it was a huge public high school with overfilled class-rooms and over four thousand students trekking through the halls. We could get away with a lot.

It was fourth period when my friend Megan started to complain:

"Ugh I don't want to go to eighth period. I haven't studied for my test at all. I'm gonna fail."

I grinned at her, grabbed my phone, and pressed one button (I had the school phone number on speed dial), then pressed the phone to my ear. I looked around the room—our teacher was all the way on the other side, blocked by a sea of rowdy students. It was fine. Stop worrying!

I put on what I thought was a bright, enthusiastic mom voice. "Hi there! This is Peggy Manzer, Megan's mom? Yeah. Megan's not gonna make it to eighth period today, she's got a bit of a tummy ache. I think it's diarrhea, but I'd rather me find out than you! Ha-ha!" I had no doubt Megan would be leaving school without a problem. My Peggy Manzer impression was spot-on.

Unfortunately, one small piece of classroom etiquette was ingrained in me despite all my efforts not to learn anything in school. Without realizing it, I was whispering on the call. I used my library voice, so it was pretty obvious that it was a student calling. Megan got detention . . . but I didn't! They never figured out it was me.

With Jack, I was the one leading us into trouble. I introduced him to his first cigarette and his first ecstasy pill. All of it. Jack kept up smoking for years after that first cigarette that I gave him. (I recently got him to quit smoking because that guilt weighed on me all this time.)

Jack went along with it all because we both felt . . . different. Also, he loved pot as much as I did. Bonding! We had this rebellious spirit that led us to shoplift and get high and hang out at the graveyard at night. There was this little section of the graveyard where an entire family was buried. The mom, the dad, and baby. Their last name was Vinkus, and our nighttime activity soon became "hanging out with the Vinkuses."

Jack's mom hated me. Can you imagine why? Because I totally can't.

She called my mom at one point and said, "I do not want your daughter anywhere near my son." We were your modern-day Homeo and Juliet: a gay boy and his troublemaker best girlfriend, torn apart by their families' disapproval of their love . . . of weed. After that we would just sneak around with our friendship. Nothing was going to split us up.

He would call my house phone over and over again, and my family couldn't stand it. He wouldn't let up until I had answered. He's actually in sales now and he's really good at it—it's that relentless persistence. But we would end up with like ten voice mails in a row, most of which were just him saying "Helloooo, Clarice" in a Hannibal Lecter voice.

As soon as I got my driver's license, our rebellious adventures entered a whole new realm. Driving us around in my parents' convertible gave us our first taste of adult freedom! Since we were two people who tended to overdo things, I'd drive with the top down and Jack would scream random things at people.

We'd drive past the elementary school around the time school got out and Jack would scream, "SANTA'S NOT REAL!!!"

We were great kids. But in this particular instance, Jack saw this really serious-looking cyclist we were passing and chose to yell, "GET OFF THE ROAD, ASSHOLE!"

The man glared at him. "Jack! That's mean," I said.

"Come on. He could have scratched your paint."

I kept driving. And then I noticed him. The biker. Following us. And he wasn't just any cyclist, this guy was the real deal, decked out in a helmet, dark shades, and jacket. And he looked fucking mad. He sped up.

"Jack . . ." I whispered, trying to stay calm.

"What?" Jack looked confused, then turned around and immediately shrank with fear. "DRIVE, BITCH, DRIVE!"

We hadn't just pissed off a random biker, we pissed off one who had apparently been pissed off FOR THE LAST TIME. Rage fueled his furious pedaling, and soon he was speeding up alongside us. I turned to try to lose him. He caught up. I turned again. There he was, pedaling on his ten-speed Schwinn, with murder in his eyes. This was the lamest car chase you'd ever see in your life. Two teens in an old convertible versus a bicyclist in the suburbs. And we were somehow losing.

I took one last turn . . . into a cul-de-sac. There was nowhere to go. The cyclist parked his bike in front of our car, and he kicked out the kickstand like a boss.

Jack, meanwhile, was hyperventilating. "Run him over! Hit him, Laura! Hit him!" And he wasn't kidding. Underneath it all, Jack has got a heart of gold . . . it's just really far underneath.

"I'm not gonna fucking hit him!" I yelled.

The cyclist slowly walked up to Jack's side of the car. He whipped off his sunglasses. With no way to escape, Jack shrank down as far as he could into his seat and rolled up the window. Of the convertible. A car with no roof.

The cyclist stared deep into Jack's eyes. Then said with raging intensity:

"May God have mercy on your soul."

Then he got back on his bike and pedaled away.

You may be wondering how a guy on a bike could have caught up to us if we were in a car. First, he was just really fast! Second, I don't speed—okay? I might have cheated in school, smoked weed, and ditched class, but the speed limit is the speed limit, you guys! After that, Jack stopped yelling at people on the street.

—

Growing up, I knew we couldn't afford things that weren't, like, food and toothpaste and clothes to cover our bodies. But I was also a teenager that existed in the world! I wanted cool makeup and tacky jewelry sometimes. So I would steal it. BUT I always justified it. It's not like I was stealing from your grandma. I would never do that! I'd steal from Walmart, a big capitalist corporation that wasn't exactly known for its good deeds. I was ethical; I had morals! I was basically Robin Hood, if he stole lip gloss from the rich and then . . . wore it.

Things got a bit more out of hand when Jack and I teamed up. We would go to the department store, take clothes into the dressing room, and then layer on everything we wanted to steal. We'd put our regular clothes back on over them and just walk out. Jack was the worst shoplifter ever. When he was nervous, he'd get these anxious, shifty eyes as he waddled out of the store with three different-colored jean hems peeking out at his ankles.

But surprisingly, we never got caught there! We were invincible. It was possible that we felt so invincible because of all the weed we were smoking. When we were high, we were totally delusional. We thought we could do anything. But that's just one theory.

24

One day, my mom gave us twenty dollars to go buy baby clothes for the neighbor's newborn. Jack and I took one look at each other. Weed money! We went straight to our dealer's house and spent the money, because—honestly—you do a better job when you don't have a backup plan.

After that, we walked inside Gymboree like confident, unremarkable adults. I even had Jack wear a pair of sunglasses to help with the shifty eyes. While Jack chatted up the cashier, I slipped a Winnie the Pooh onesie under my jacket. Then we were out of there, no problem. Brilliant! After a series of high fives, Jack and I absolutely had to smoke a bowl in the car to celebrate. We had talent.

We arrived home very high and handed my mother the onesie, still on the hanger, with no bag or receipt. A bit of paranoia was starting to kick in. She examined the garment and eyed both of us. *Oh shit. She knows she knows she knows . . . don't make eye contact . . . she knows sh—*

"It's too big, Laura."

"Huh?"

"This is a six-to-eight-month size. I said zero-to-six-months size."

"The baby is going to grow into it, right?"

"Do you want her to think that we think her baby is fat?"

I was too high to even comprehend that last sentence. I stared at her, squinting my swollen eyes.

"Just exchange it. Please."

"No problemo, mamacita." I grabbed the onesie back, and Jack and I walked out of there.

You can't return a stolen item, so we'd just have to steal again . . . twenty minutes after the first time. Is this what they refer to as "spiraling out of control"? Perhaps!

We made it back into the Gymboree. On this caper, there was no time to chat up the cashier. We had to get in and out, unnoticed.

I lunged to pull Jack's sunglasses over his eyes.

"Stop—stop it! Don't touch my hair!"

The cashier spotted us. "Oh hey! Back again so soon."

Jack panicked. "Yeah, well! We had some second thoughts and we know our little diva is going to want a selection of—"

"I'm hungry let's go!" I interrupted, onesie already in my purse.

"Byeeeee!" Jack waved and we were gone.

The cashier watched us leave, confused. This whole debacle just confirmed that we were geniuses. Maybe our teachers didn't see it, and our grades didn't reflect it, but we were fucking smart and we were going to smoke another bowl to celebrate. But then the bowl was clogged. Good thing we had the wrong-size onesie to clean it out!

In our super high state, we totally forgot to discard the resin-covered onesie. My mom found it a couple days later in the back of the car. Or more likely, she probably smelled the stale drugs first. Finding out that the source of the smell was a Winnie the Pooh resin-smeared onesie was just the cherry on top, I'm sure!

That sounds bad, I agree. But I want to clarify that I wasn't the "bad seed" in a perfect town. As I got older, the polished veneer of Downers Grove started to fade away, blemish by blemish. Suburbs aren't immune from bad things! Some people there were just completely fucked up.

At the high school down the road, the school librarian, (the mother of a friend of mine, I might add), fucked like seventeen different high school boys. She'd leave notes in the books for them, detailing when and where to meet. Honestly, it sounds like she got the idea from a terrible rom-com. People started to notice something was awry when all the boys at school started clamoring to hang out in the library. Like, how is there a line to get in? And then the boys started gossiping with one another.

"Yo dude, don't tell anyone, but I banged the librarian!"

"Wait. *I* banged the librarian."

"Wait . . . but . . . so did *I*." Aaaaand cue terrible moment of recognition that everyone had banged her.

But back to my story. I love my liberal hippie parents, and I love the values I was raised with, but looking back it's clear I could have used a bit more structure. A few more consequences. Well, I guess they DID tell me to stop getting arrested. And the rest of the world DID try to slam me with consequences over and over again, whether it was my grades, or detention, or getting arrested for marijuana possession. Geez. Okay, maybe I just didn't listen.

When I was fifteen, a few of my friends and I rented a motel room so that we could party in PEACE. Also known as . . . a place we could get wasted and high without our parents finding out. Things started to get rowdy, and soon enough, the cops knocked on our door. GREAT.

"We've received a noise complaint about your gathering here and we're gonna need you to quiet down or disperse."

Now, I was wasted. At this time, I didn't know liquid courage was a thing. I thought I was just really fucking brave all the time. I was going to save us from the cops.

I'll have you know that I did learn a few things in school. I found my psychology class particularly interesting. The better I knew how other people thought, the more easily I could steal and lie and get away with it.

The cops were only there on a noise complaint, but I grabbed my purse and slurred at them: "You want to check my purse?? Go ahead! Check it! Check it! I have nothing to hide!"

I smiled smugly. They were NEVER gonna check my purse, BECAUSE I asked them to. That's what reverse psychology is! The two cops looked at each other and shrugged.

"Okay."

They grabbed my purse and started to sift through it. The first cop lifted out a baggie of weed.

"Aaaaand . . . You're under arrest."

He enjoyed his job way too much.

After that, they made me go to something called Self-Management Skills class. Have you seen that show *Scared Straight*? It was exactly that. A bunch of other bad kids and I did a full tour of a women's jail. And—oh cool!—the librarian I mentioned earlier was there, serving her eight years!

"Hey Mrs. Renworth! What's up!" She didn't respond.

After the tour we were separated into prison cells in order to be screamed at individually by a prisoner. I got paired with an ex-junky with especially colorful language and not enough teeth to ably pronounce all the words she was yelling at me. I came out of that program with a detailed knowledge of the prison's layout and a bunch of new drug connects and friends that liked getting into trouble. It was awesome.

Through it all, I had a plan. I was going to graduate high school (although even graduating itself seemed a bit unnecessary at times), and then I was going to move to LA to be an actress. For me, it was written in the stars ever since the moment that I saw Maggie's older sister in a high school play!

I'll have you know I was good at acting. How did I know at only age fifteen, you ask? It's a valid question. Downers Grove was fairly small, and I had only done high school theater and speech. But I knew I had a knack for making people laugh and making people believe me. I just combined my desire to do illegal things with my ability to become anyone.

In the absence of an actual agent or manager or sitcom to star in, the world was my stage, and I was casting myself.

My friend Andy Junk and I did theater and improv together, and we shared the desire to take acting to the next level. One time we went to a real estate open house in town pretending to be a pair of southern newlyweds, complete with terrible accents. We stared at every aspect of the house, acting really impressed because it was so much nicer than our respective mamas' houses.

The bubbly real estate agent hopped over to us and started to chat us up.

"Don't you two love the house?"

I smiled at her. "Yes, it's so much nicer than Mama's house back in Georgia!"

The real estate agent hugged her clipboard to her body as she leaned into the conversation. "Oh, I'm so glad to hear that! What part of Georgia are you from? I have family in Atlanta."

"Down in . . . near the mountain—"

The agent nodded. "Do you two have any kids?"

Then, SIMULTANEOUSLY:

Andy responded: "Nope!"

While I responded: "Six!"

We looked at each other, wide eyed, struggling to explain. "Um . . . I . . ."

Andy stammered, "I . . . don't have . . . per se . . ."

I finally thought of it. "Sorry. It's just a sore spot for us. The six are mine. I have six kids. From different men. Andy here is just recently in the picture." I grinned.

"Yes! She's a bit of a whore," Andy confirmed with a big thumbs-up.

"Oh . . . kay." She left us alone after that. Success, kind of!

Another time, Jack and I wanted cigarettes, but we were both underage and had no money. Just a few hurdles there. I've always felt that where there's a will there's a way. (Is it still a positive attitude if you're using it to do bad things?) Think, Laura, think: *How are we going to get cigarettes without getting carded?*

I've got it!

I drove us to the gas station and parked off to the side. I turned to Jack. "Walk into the store, and when I come in, pretend like you don't know me."

I looked in the mirror and smeared my eyeliner down my cheeks to look distressed, as if I had been crying.

Jack smiled. "Ooooh, she's getting messy for this one!" And then, quieter, "Um . . . Is there a plan or—"

"Go go go!" I pushed him out of the car.

I waited three minutes and then sprinted into the gas station convenience store, out of breath, and started sobbing onto the cashier's counter. Jack was at the pop machine, filling up a soda while he watched me, wide eyed.

"I don't know what to do! Oh my God, oh my God—my boyfriend just left me! He just drove away with my ID and all my money and everything I own!" I was bawling and hyperventilating.

The cashier looked very taken aback. He leaned as far away as he could from my sobbing body, and reached out from a distance to pat me lightly on the arm. "Oh, ma'am . . . I am so sorry . . . Is there anything I can do? I'm so—please stop crying onto the counter, ma'am. What can I do?"

I sniffled and looked up at him gratefully.

"Well . . . I could use some menthol lights."

"Yes, yes okay, here." The cashier grabbed them for me.

"And a lighter. Thanks. No, no, the pink one."

The cashier grabbed that for me, too. I sniffled gratefully. "Bless you. I feel so much better."

"No problem, ma'am, I'm so sorry to hear about your boyfriend—"

"Thanks!" I waved and walked away. He didn't even card me.

Once we were outside, Jack grabbed my arm. "BITCH, ARE YOU KIDDING ME? That deserved an Oscar!"

"I know, right?" Then I lit up both our cigarettes.

It's true that I did things like this to get what I wanted, but I was also addicted to the thrill of it. The adrenaline, the risk. I think it's my addict personality. It was dangerous, high stakes, and there was always something appealing about that to me. It's most people's worst nightmare, but it was what I thrived on.

Many years later, in an Alcoholics Anonymous meeting, I met a woman who worked in the ER of a children's hospital. She said to me, casually, "Yeah, children come in every day, age twelve and attempted suicide! And I have about five minutes to save their lives, if that." She sighed dreamily, "I love my job!" I just stared at her, dumbfounded. Holy shit, right? How can a person live with that kind of pressure, let alone love it? But she thrived in those life-or-death, high-stakes situations. At least she channeled her addiction to that thrill into something positive.

Saving lives is a slightly more productive use of that energy than stealing menthol lights.

Theater was my only source of relief at high school. I loved it and I tried hard during that class. I had the opposite perspective of most of my fellow classmates: the ticket to my future was not in chemistry or math or science—it was in theater rehearsals and the plays we put on. I took these seriously. Because of that, my theater coach, Mrs. Heiteen, was the only adult at school that liked me and saw potential in me—even when my GPA was falling down faster than a freshman doing shots.

During my senior year, when all my friends started getting into college and making plans for their futures, Mrs. Heiteen took a look at my grades. She approached me, very angry.

"Damn it, Laura. You fucked yourself out of 90 percent of the colleges in the country. And is that weed I smell in your purse?"

She was correct on both counts. No college was going to let an idiot teenager with a multiple-arrest history, failing grades, and a penchant for drunken idiocy onto their campus. And there was a lot of weed in my purse.

I truly didn't care, because I was going to be an actress—there was no plan B! Luckily, I was very good at it. Because of that, it was the only thing I put effort into, besides finding drugs and places to do drugs. Let's just say it was my only positive obsession.

I had joined the speech team during my freshman year. Speech is like competitive acting. You perform eight minutes of a play as one person or a duet, and then eventually compete with kids at other high schools in the area. If you're good enough, you go to the state competition; and if you're really, really good, you compete in nationals. It was a big deal, you guys. Especially to me.

On the first day of speech, we did Humorous Duet Acting. Mrs. Heiteen paired me with Tina, this socially awkward girl with pants ever so slightly too short. Tina was one of the girls that The Twelve had chosen to bully in junior high. She didn't like me, and I didn't know how I was going to be able to reach my comedic-genius potential with this dorky girl on my ass. We were going to have to rehearse together for months! So . . . fuck. Really, Mrs. Heiteen? Really?

But I have never been more wrong. We worked together day after day, and I realized she was one of the most hilarious people I've ever met. She was sweet and witty and so smart. And I just fell in love with being her friend. We became so close after that.

When I started taking speech seriously, it felt like I was working for my career to happen. I was memorizing the monologues I saw on television and in movies. I was trekking into the city with Andy Junk to take courses at The Second City. See? I knew how to focus . . . just not on US History. I tried my best in those Second City classes, but I still hated them. Even though comedy and acting were what I wanted to do, any sort of class made me feel stupid and not good enough to be there. Something about being in a class environment automatically made all my insecurities come out. I much preferred improv on the street with unsuspecting civilians.

The annual speech competition came around. I wanted to be ready. There was a category called Original Comedy, where you play all the characters in a comedic eight-minute play that you wrote. This was MY territory. I wrote a piece called *Pink Slip*, about a group of oddball students who got detention. For the first time, I was doing well at something in school.

I performed *Pink Slip* at regionals and won first place. Mrs. Heiteen ran up to me and gave me an awkward high five—the highest form of approval from her. I couldn't stop smiling, holding my dinky medal. I remember thinking, *Wait a second. Does . . . hard work . . . pay off????? Holy shit.*

At the same time, I was battling my need to get high. When I was winning speech, I was winning against my demons. I was still smoking and drinking, but I was balancing it with my work because I had something important to focus on.

As the state competition got closer, Mrs. Heiteen became my personal coach—egging me on to focus, to practice, to stay clear. I could win this. She said I could; I knew I could. I was good, and people were finally going to see that. I would finally be on my way to the career I was meant for.

And then . . .

I won state. First place!

There was only one more step. Taking on nationals.

In the week leading up to nationals, I took a break from rehearsing and went out one night to dinner with Jack and our other friend, Kaylen. We were smoking cigarettes and chatting. Side note: Did you know smoking was allowed indoors in 2004? Maybe that was just a Midwest thing, but there was a smoking section at the Omega Diner.

One of the teachers at my school was there, too. She saw me smoking and reported me to the school.

The next day in theater class Mrs. Heiteen approached me, looking more angry than usual. Or maybe it was sad. She told me I was disqualified from nationals for smoking last night, *in the fucking diner.* Of all the substances to be disqualified for, it was cigarettes—the least illegal of my vices!

I was disqualified from the one thing I had going for me.

I didn't cry about it. I got high with Jack instead.

Mrs. Heiteen still made me go to nationals in Salt Lake City, Utah, just to watch. I saw every other student perform, wishing I was in their place, knowing I could have rocked this. Then I convinced some Mormon dudes to buy Tina and me beer. We got drunk with them in our hotel room.

Speech was the one thing I had been holding on to . . . and I felt like it let go of me. So I let go, too. I began to spiral.

I was fifteen when I got high and drunk and had sex with a guy who was eighteen, at least, and also high on 'shrooms. He was such an asshole.

The room was pitch-black. It was his room. I told him to put a condom on, please. He said okay. He walked over to his nightstand. He opened the drawer and then closed it. He paused, putting it on. Then he had sex with me.

A few weeks later I started throwing up in the mornings, and not because I was hungover. Fuck!

At the same time, I was playing the pregnant Virgin Mary in the school play. No joke. At rehearsals I had to wear a fake pregnancy belly over my actual pregnant belly. Talk about too real.

"Um, Laura, your portrayal of Mary is a bit more . . . anxious than necessary, perhaps?"

"Well, Mary didn't ask for this baby, Mrs. Heiteen!"

I wondered if God had lied to Mary about putting a condom on.

I asked the guy who got me pregnant for three hundred dollars, half the cost of an abortion. I thought it was only fair that he paid for half of it. Even though there was nothing really fair about this at all.

The kicker is that he made me meet him at a White Castle restaurant bathroom and pee on a pregnancy test in front of him to make sure I wasn't lying. He thought I was trying to get "abortion money" from him. He said that like it was a thing.

Since when is "abortion money" a thing? It's NOT a thing. If a guy thinks there is a pattern of girls scamming him out of "abortion money," then he really needs to reevaluate his actions. Like, damn!

He took a look at the two lines on my pee stick, handed me the money, and left. No words. I never talked to him again.

I added it to my own three hundred dollars and headed to Planned Parenthood with my friend Nicole. Nicole was another outcast with Jack and me. She was really smart, openly bisexual, very punk. I knew she wouldn't judge me . . . and that she would be able to handle the protesters.

There were rows of them outside the clinic. Pro-life women yelling at me.

"You know your baby has fingers, right? It has a heartbeat!"

"How could you kill your own child? How could you be so self-ish?"

I looked down as I passed them. Nicole stopped.

"Nicole. Come on."

"Well, her baby's actually, like, super gay, so you guys would probably want to abort that one, huh?"

That was the only thing that got me to smile that day.

I didn't tell my parents, even though I was really close to my mom. I was too scared.

A week or so later, she found prescription painkillers in my room.

She asked me gently, "Did you get breast implants?"

I stared at her, confused. Then looked down. Oh. My boobs had gotten way bigger from all the pregnancy hormones. I thought up a lie.

I stuttered, "No . . . no I didn't but . . . my friend Dani got an abortion and didn't want her parents to find out, so I told her she could do it in my name." The best lies have a grain of truth in them, right?

And yet, I know, not my finest work. Why would I have my friend's pills? It's idiotic. My mom just kind of looked at me sadly and nodded. Years later she asked if it was actually me who got the abortion. I finally told her the truth. She began to cry, and said, "I just wish I could have been there for you through that. I would have supported you. You didn't have to lie."

I wished I hadn't.

—

A year later, when I was sixteen, some good news came. There was a new TV show holding auditions around the country. It was going to be like *American Idol*, but for acting! Contestants had to prepare a monologue and audition in front of the judges.

This was going to be my big break, the thing that launched my career! I mean, it worked for Kelly Clarkson and a bunch of other people whose names I don't remember on *American Idol*!

I learned a monologue. I was so serious about it that I didn't even smoke weed the day before the audition. THAT'S how much I cared.

I studied my ass off. It was like speech all over again. My monologue was hilarious, and I knew I was going to nail it. I took the train to Chicago where the auditions were being held, and stood in line for hours and hours. When I finally got in front of the judges, I had them in stitches. I was on cloud nine.

One of the producers, who looked to be in his forties, pulled me off to the side.

"Laura, right? You were brilliant."

I said, "Oh, you think so? That's so nice of you." But I was thinking, *You're damn right I was.*

He smiled charmingly. "We should meet tonight and talk about opportunities for you in Los Angeles. We want you to be on the show."

YES. Yes yes yes. My sixteen-year-old brain could not even fathom my dreams coming true right now, in this moment.

I trekked home, swung open the door, and yelled, "HELLO, FAMILY! I'VE MADE IT."

My dad looked up from the couch. "That's right, honey! You're amazing!"

I found my mother and Colleen in the dining room and filled them in. They needed to enjoy my company now, because my time in Downers Grove would be fleeting, as I would soon be a star and have forgotten about them completely.

"It's called a second meeting, and only the best actors get them. We're going to talk about my career."

Colleen gasped. "That's great!"

I feigned confidence, but I was nervous. I didn't know how to conduct myself in professional late-night meetings!

"Can you come with me, Colleen?"

Colleen drove me to the W Hotel that night. Oh, did I mention his meeting spot of choice was the W Hotel?

I found him at the bar. Colleen sat off to the side of the bar and watched.

"Here. Have a drink, Laura."

"Have another drink."

"Have another."

I just kept drinking what he gave me. I didn't want to be rude. I had to get to LA and I kept thinking that this was my ticket, this was how the industry worked. It was getting later and later.

Colleen tapped me on the shoulder. "I want to go home, Laura. Can we go?"

We moved out of earshot of the producer.

"I think I have to stay," I said.

Colleen was annoyed. "Well, if you have to stay, then stay. I'm going home. I have work in the morning."

I sighed. "Okay, fine." I would take the train home. I went back to the producer . . . and I don't remember anything after that. I blacked out completely.

I woke up in the morning to the sun glaring on my face. Squinting in the bright morning light, I looked around. I was in an empty hotel room. There was forty dollars next to me, and a note that read: *Thanks for last night. Here's money for a cab.*

I didn't even get on the show.

Colleen got a DUI on the way home. So, lose-lose.

At this point I was just ready to leave my town, to go anywhere but here. I hated school and I hated getting in trouble and it felt like that was all I was doing.

After acting out in one of my classes, I was brought in to see the school counselor. I remember wondering why I wasn't just being punished like usual.

"Is everything okay at home?" The counselor looked at me with understanding.

I looked at him and narrowed my eyes. "Can I just have detention?"

I didn't really know what to say. He recommended therapy for me.

I brought it up to my mom that night. I told her that I maybe thought it was kind of a good idea. Maybe there is something going on with me and I could talk to someone and get better.

"If you need to talk to someone, you can talk to me."

It was one of two things. First of all, we never, ever went to the doctor. We didn't have health insurance growing up. So she might have thought that there was no fucking way we could afford therapy for me, which was completely valid. She also might have not wanted to expose what was going on at home.

I liked my home life. I loved my parents. But I suppose the unsettling thing at home for me was my dad's drinking. It could be scary at times. He didn't beat us or anything like that, but he was six four, and he could get so angry. Like throwing-glass-at-the-wall, breaking-things sort of angry. The scary part was that we'd never really know which dad we were gonna get. He could be a nice, funny, supportive drunk that I loved so much, or a mean and angry drunk. But very consistently, drunk.

One time I called him to pick me up from a restaurant in town. When he arrived, he was noticeably drunk. The mean, angry kind. He was so mad that I asked him to come get me that he was driving 80 mph on the suburban streets while slurring insults at me. He swerved onto our neighbors' lawn, barely missing the lampposts, and almost hit the house. I remember sprinting out of the car, into the house, and locking myself in my room. I thought he was mad enough to kill me.

My mom, however, was so loving, she really made up for it.

I was scared, but my dad was not a monster by any means. He was sick. He was stuck in his disease. When he was sober, he was this funny, creative musician and scientist. Always pushing us to

40

think outside the box and be ourselves, no matter who that was. He taught me to question the status quo in a way that I am so grateful about today.

I'm not complaining about my childhood or where I've been, but I can see how that would have caused me to act out. I can see now how much pain I was holding. I would sleep with a knife next to my bed, because for some reason it soothed me to know that if I wanted to, I could just grab it and end it all for myself. (Admittedly, it *was* a butter knife. . . .) I once took six of my mother's sleeping pills. I passed out and got really sick from them, but I was going to live.

You know, if I was really trying to kill myself, I would have taken the whole bottle of pills or chosen a sharper knife. Six pills and a butter knife were not gonna take me out.

I decided to channel my emotions into finding ways to escape my reality, through drinking or smoking or, even better, both. The kids in my town needed a new place to party after getting in trouble for all our motel parties, but no fear, my friends were problem solvers when it came to getting fucked up. So they chose the next best option—breaking into our friend's house while his family was on vacation!

Okay, not so legal, but I didn't care. It wasn't my party and I wasn't getting in trouble for it. A boy named Richard invited me, and while I barely even knew him, I wasn't about to say no to free booze and weed. I took him up on the invite, and obviously brought along Jack and our friend Holly.

Once I got there, this five-foot-tall girl in a strapless top and miniskirt ('oos fashion, amirite?) came up to me. "So you're Laura Clery?"

I had never seen this girl in my life. I was already six feet tall by now, so I looked down at her—literally—and said, "Yeah?"

And then BOOM! She punched me in the nose. Honestly, like, how did she even reach my nose? She tackled me to the ground and started beating the shit out of me. But she was so much smaller than me that I put up my fists and took her down like she was nothing.

No, I'm totally kidding.

I'm not a fighter at all! I was just screaming and crying and taking it and begging her to stop.

Some of the other kids at the party grabbed her and pulled her off me. Jack and Holly and I ran into the bathroom and locked the door.

"Who the fuck was that?"

"Richard's ex-girlfriend."

Seriously?? Seriously????? She was *that* mad because her ex-boyfriend invited me to a party????

I was furious. I started pacing around the bathroom. How could she do that to me? I felt like I was a tetherball being slapped around a pole. There was nothing in my life that I had control over.

I looked up and saw this painting of a boat on the bathroom wall. Just a boat floating on the water. I saw my own face reflected faintly on the glass. My fucking black eye and bloody nose.

I punched it as hard as I could. Glass shattered everywhere, including into my hand and wrist. It hit some major veins, and blood was gushing everywhere. I slumped down, crying.

Holly immediately jumped into action, picking out the pieces of glass. She rinsed it with water. Jack wrapped the wound in his shirt. How convenient that we were already in a bathroom.

We didn't go to the hospital, even though I knew we should have. The avoidance of hospitals was something I had inherited from my parents. Plus, I didn't want to get in trouble—we had all been drinking. We just bought some bandages and wrapped me up, and I went home at two a.m.

There was my dad sitting on his La-Z-Boy, red wine in hand.

"Who did that to you? I'll fucking kill him!"

"It's fine, Dad."

Richard, who invited me, did eventually apologize for the whole thing.

"My ex is a crazy bitch, right? Ha-ha."

I'd just stared at him until it got uncomfortable for him. "We are not bonding over this right now."

"Sorry about that," he'd said awkwardly.

That family who owned the house we broke into returned home eventually . . . and saw a bunch of fun things all around their house! Empty bottles of alcohol. Cigarette butts. Oh yeah, and BLOOD AND GLASS ALL OVER THEIR BATHROOM.

It was on the news one night. "A house in Hinsdale was broken into while that family was away on vacation. There is evidence of physical violence and property damage, although nothing was stolen."

"Mom! Dad! That's my blood on the TV! That's my blood!" I was so desperate to be on TV that even my blood making an appearance on the seven o'clock news was an accomplishment.

That night, Holly had left her phone in the bathroom. The tiny girl who beat me up found it. I started getting texts from her. I know what you're thinking, and no, she didn't want to go for coffee. I was surprised too!

You have 2 hours to get us 500 dollars. Or else we're smashing this phone.

Clearly, they wanted us to pay for the damage we caused in the bathroom.

It would honestly be cheaper for Holly to buy a new phone. Sorry, Holly.

1 hour left.

30 minutes.

15 minutes.

Geez. She didn't need to text that frequently. I knew how to read time!

When it had finally been two hours . . . she sent one last text.

It's Hammer Time.

IT'S HAMMER TIME??? Never have I heard that joyous exclamation used in such a menacing way.

Next time I really want to instill fear in someone, I'm going to try a deep stare into their eyes and whisper, "It's *Hammer Time*. (Oh-oh oh oh oh-oh-oh)."

The time it really was, though? Time for me to get out of Downers Grove.

CHAPTER 3

My Summer of (possibly too much) Freedom

My senior year of high school, I was voted Most Likely to Be Late to Graduation. Which is rude! I was totally on time.

I already mentioned that I had to take geometry three times, right? Well, the third time was my senior year of high school. And if I didn't pass . . . I was staying another year. I barely, barely passed—and the only reason I did was because my oldest sister, Tracy, is a high school math teacher and she coached me through it. So in defense of the title I won, I very well could have been late to graduation: a year late!

BUT I WASN'T. Let's focus on that.

I walked across that freaking stage at graduation and said my final "fuck you" to that godforsaken place. I was finally ready to get to LA and do what I was MEANT to do. Acting!

There was only one problem. I had no plan at all. And no money. And no job lined up.

Cool.

Oddly, I had this unshakable faith that I was going to make it. Some might call me delusional, but I'd rather think of it as trust. Faith. Blind faith! Becoming an actress was my destiny, and when someone has a destiny, it always comes true. Right? Okay, now that I'm saying it out loud I can hear how delusional I sound. Maybe I was delusional! But! . . . Look at where I am now—living the dream.

When my opportunity to move to LA came, I was slightly surprised. I got a call from Neha, a girl who I did speech with. Neha graduated a year before me and was going to Northwestern now. She had it together in high school, so she got in. Good for her.

"Neesie and I are going to LA this summer. I'm interning at a production company and she's going to stay with me for fun. Come out with us! I know you want to."

I gasped. "Oh God, this is it."

Neha continued, "I mean, you'd have to pay rent and stuff, and I know flying out there can be pricey so you can take some time to think about it—"

"I'M THERE. WHEN? TOMORROW? OH WAIT, I HAVE TO GRADUATE THIS WEEK. CRAP. FUCK IT, THEY WON'T MISS ME. I CAN COME TOMORROW."

"Dude, not tomorrow."

"Right."

"You don't have to ask your parents?"

"Who?"

I didn't even ask my parents if I could go. I knew they'd be fine with it. Instead I simply told them I was leaving.

"Bye, Mom and Dad! I'm off to follow my acting dreams in Los Angeles without any practical steps or a plan!"

46

"Have fun, honey!"

"You can do it, you're amazing!"

They did not have the same perspective that most traditional parents did. They never tried to steer me toward a more practical, steady career. I have so many friends who got discouraged from their art by their parents before they even had a chance to try. They had to hear things like "Do you know the odds of you making it?" and "How are you going to support a family with that?" So they never even attempted it. My parents were the opposite. They'd say, "If you want to act, then do it. Life is short."

Honestly I'm so grateful that they had this mindset. Yes, I lived a bit dangerously for a while, but I firmly believe that if I ever gave myself a plan B, an exit door from my dreams, I wouldn't have been able to become a full-time working actress by twenty-three. I would have taken the exit. Reaching your potential is fucking scary.

I still had the money issue to solve, though. Luckily, my family believed in me just as much as I did. Colleen was earning some money working at a restaurant at this time, so she and my mother both put in money to help me pay for rent and the plane ticket. This was happening!

I knew that Neha and Neesie were only going to LA for the summer, but I wasn't planning on coming back to Downers Grove! If I had found a way to get myself out there, I knew I would find a way to stay.

Just days after graduation, I flew straight to LA.

I stayed with Neha and Neesie on their living room couch. I was perpetually out of money and never knew how I was going to pay for my next meal! It was the most fun summer of my life thus far. My first taste of real ADULTHOOD. Which to me was . . . partying.

Don't get me wrong, I came to LA with the intention of getting my acting career started. But it was like unleashing a kid in a candy store. Except . . . more like an addict in a drug store. I mean, a store filled with drugs. Not, like, CVS. An addict in CVS would probably be fine.

Like I said, I knew I was going to make it . . . but seventeen-year-old Laura thought that this meant I didn't have to work for it. That success would just find me. That's how life worked, right? #notatalldelusional.

While I was waiting for my million-dollar movie deal, I had to do SOMETHING, so Neesie and I would smoke weed every day and go out to clubs every night. (Meanwhile Neha was busy focusing hard at her internship and being somewhat responsible.) We were staying in Westwood, a total college town, so there were frat parties galore. I met enough frat guys that summer to get the complete college experience.

When it came to acting, I had no idea what I was doing. I kind of figured that in Hollywood, you just had to look beautiful and go to a department store. Some major producer would discover your insane talent while you purchased a silk scarf. Or in my case, while I walked out of Macy's with three pairs of pants layered under my jeans.

I had one friend in town who knew a manager. She offered to pass on my headshot and résumé. Sorry, what? I didn't have either of those.

"You need a résumé if anyone is going to consider signing you."

Okay. I found some dodgy modeling photos I had taken back in Downers Grove with an amateur photographer, complete with fake tan and incredibly skinny eyebrows. I also was bleaching my teeth with dollar-store teeth whitener, so I had white bleach spots all over my gums. Hello, world!

And résumé-wise . . . I wrote it out by hand. By HAND. I want you to know that I had access to a printer, but did not use it. Instead I chose to whip out my ten-year-old-boy handwriting to really nail my professionalism as I wrote: *Special skills include horseback riding, driving a car, and a Macedonian accent.*

On that résumé I made a bunch of shit up. I knew that a list of high school plays was not going to impress a real life LA manager! So I added some fake local community theater productions as well. Boom! Ready to knock their socks off.

I handed it to my friend to pass along.

"Dude. This isn't legible at all."

". . ."

Thankfully, she had much neater handwriting than I did, so she rewrote the whole thing more legibly. (But can someone tell me why we didn't just go to the library and print it??? Why did we not think of that?)

Suffice it to say, I did not get a meeting with that manager.

I wasn't exactly getting any auditions, but so what? I didn't need auditions. I was MEETING people. LA is really stratified during the day. At nine a.m., the movie executives take their elevators to the twenty-sixth floor of their skyscraper offices and the unemployed actors smoke weed in their apartments (right?). But at night, we all drank at the same bars and danced on the same dance floors until three a.m. See? There's a bit of community in having a cocaine problem.

The day might be filled with rejections, but at night, people loved me.

One night, I was standing outside the Argyle at two a.m., smoking a cigarette. This really pretty boy approaches me. Damn. Is he . . . prettier than me?

He came over to me. "You're gorgeous," he said.

"Oh God, you too," I blurted out.

"Oh, thanks. You should be a model."

I gasped, flattered, but the cigarette in my mouth made me cough a little. "Really? You think so?"

"Yes. I would love to shoot you."

"Um . . . with a camera, right?"

"Ha-ha! Wow. You're funny, too."

But seriously, with a camera, right? Right?? His name was Damon. He gave me some cocaine, so I gave him my number. And just like that, I became a professional model. Well, not actually, but if you had tried to convince me otherwise, I wouldn't have heard it. That's the LA dream for you right there!

On one night out I met an agent from Endeavor with a huge cocaine problem. This was my chance to sell my talent to him.

"You don't understand. I've got what it takes. I'm the next Charlize Theron."

"Really?"

"Absolutely. Give me a script and I will fucking destroy it. I'll interpret the shit out of it. You think you've seen real acting before, but you haven't until you've seen me."

I think they typically call this liquid courage, but in my case it was powdered.

"All right. I'm sold. Call me next week." He handed me his business card.

And *that's* how it's done, bitches.

Although I was the slightest bit worried he was too high when we met to remember me at all. I gave him a call anyway, trying to channel the same confidence I'd had that night.

"Of course I remember you, Laura!" he exclaimed.

Oh thank God.

"I got you an audition for *X-Men*!"

My mouth went dry with fear. Excuse me? *X-Men*? Let me remind you that I'd never had a real professional audition in my life. And I was supposed to jump straight into *X-Men*?

"Perfect. That is perfect for me."

"Great. We'll see how you do on this audition and then we'll talk about your future."

"You won't be disappointed!"

Oh, fuck.

In the daytime, my fearlessness drained away. It was like in the dark of night I couldn't see all the things I was afraid of. Nighttime Laura really liked to fuck over daytime Laura. Mostly it was just hangovers and no energy at all, but this? This audition? This was terrifying.

I prepped as hard as I could. I learned the sides forward and backward, and then I got nervous that I would accidentally do them backward, so I repeated them forward twenty more times. I knew I couldn't give myself any excuse not to show up. When I walked into the casting office, I was ready to give the performance of my life.

It was a basically empty room, except for a table, a camera, a few producers, and the casting director. The casting director smiled at me. "Okay, Laura, we've heard great things. I'll be reading the lines with you. You ready?"

Say yes, Laura. Say yes. Say something. I was petrified. I think I just opened my eyes really wide and nodded. That's normal.

She read the first line to me: "I'm the wrong guy to play hide and seek with."

I took a breath and LOOKED STRAIGHT INTO THE CAMERA. "Who's hiding, dickhead."

The casting director glanced awkwardly at the producers as I

MAINTAINED EYE CONTACT WITH THE CAMERA LIKE AN IDIOT. She continued on.

I gave my entire reading staring into the lens.

Can you guys imagine watching a movie where every character looks straight into the camera the whole time? It's not exactly what they were going for.

That is the most rookie mistake someone could ever make. I just imagine the director watching the tapes later, uncomfortably trying to avoid the super-intense big-eye glare of a girl more nervous than anyone has been in the history of the world. Or laughing his ass off. Most likely that.

I didn't know how to audition! I had no idea that it was even something I needed to learn how to do.

By the way, the part was Kitty Pryde in *X-Men: The Last Stand*. Ellen Page plays her in all the movies, and she didn't look into the camera even once. So, good choice everybody.

The coke-problem agent called me shortly after the audition. "So . . . I got some notes back from the casting director."

"Oh great!" Lay it on me, buster. I can handle it.

"She just said . . . your client needs auditioning classes."

After this, he didn't want to represent me. Who knows why?

Let's just say this was a humbling experience. I realized that there was a craft I needed to learn if I actually wanted to book jobs. And I did take some auditioning classes.

I'm only slightly embarrassed to say that this was the highest point of my career during my first stint in LA. But at the time, I wasn't embarrassed at all! I felt fucking successful, going on auditions and shit, and successfully getting high every day. I was solid.

Toward the end of the summer, things started to get more and more out of control. Neha, Neesie, and I ran out of money. We had already paid rent, luckily, but money to eat? Not so plentiful.

No worries! I had skills for this. I knew how to get free stuff! I trained my whole life for this.

I pulled into the In-N-Out drive-thru with Neesie, fully aware that neither of us had any money. She was not down. "What the fuck are you doing, Laura?"

"Chill out. I got this, okay? I got this. Just order. They're going to give it to us."

Neesie looked at me skeptically. Hey, save the skepticism for conspiracy theories! I pulled up to the window and we ordered. And then came time to pay.

I patted my pockets EXCESSIVELY. And then dug through my purse. "Oh shit. Oh shit, where's my wallet? Oh my God, did someone steal it?" I looked at the cashier for any hint of sympathy. There was none whatsoever. Damn. LA was definitely not the Midwest.

Neesie was getting worried. "Hold on one second," I said. I put the car in park, walked over to the dudes in the car behind us.

"Hey, I'm SO sorry. But I can't find my wallet and I already ordered . . . could I borrow some money?"

The dudes were super annoyed. But they paid. And we lived another day!

I began to realize my trusty stealing methods really didn't fly in LA. But am I the type of person to give up?? No!

Meantime, I had given myself some scars on my lower stomach from an at-home bikini wax gone wrong (do those *ever* go right?). Because I was not really feeling up to rock some vagina scars, I needed to get some scar cream. I went to the CVS on La Brea and Santa Monica and found the creams. There was one for five dollars . . .

but there was also one for forty dollars. I could have easily bought the five-dollar one. But the forty-dollar one was probably better. I mean, why else would it cost that much?? I wanted it. I needed it. I deserved the best.

Years later in Alcoholics Anonymous, I learned that this is a trait of the alcoholic. It's either grandiose or comatose. Either *I'm the best and deserve the best!* or *I'm a piece of shit and I'm killing myself tonight!* Once you're sober, you practice learning that you're no better or worse than anyone else. But in this moment . . . I was feeling grandiose.

I slipped the forty-dollar scar cream into my purse and walked out.

The manager was this big, angry man. You could tell that he had been pissed off for the last fucking time today as he followed me to the exit.

"HEY! STOP! One of my employees saw you put something in your purse. What did you take?"

This was not a man I wanted to pick a fight with. I immediately pulled out the scar cream.

"I'm so sorry, I'm so sorry. I took your scar cream. I couldn't afford it and I have scars from something I don't want to talk about and if you were a woman you would understand, but here it is, take it, I'm so sorry. Please. I'll just go."

He snatched the cream back and eyed me. I could tell he wished I had resisted more. He really wanted to yell at someone.

"What else do you have in there?"

"Just that, I swear."

Then, I'm sure he thought, *Fuck it, might as well just yell at this seventeen-year-old!* He turned to the twenty-five people waiting in line to check out.

"HEY, EVERYONE. LOOK WHO DECIDED TO SHOPLIFT TODAY? MISS—What's your name?"

"Laura."

"LAURA WANTED SCAR CREAM!!" Everyone in line looked at me pityingly. The manager turned back to me. "Get out of here."

I walked out of that CVS with my head down, a walk of shame more humiliating than ANY of the times I had come home at eight a.m. in my clubbing dress. I crossed the street as fast as I could, but then I heard police sirens. The manager had called the cops on me.

"HANDS OVER YOUR HEAD. HANDS OVER YOUR HEAD."

Are you fucking kidding me?

I was in front of the busiest Starbucks in LA, leaned against a cop car. My most public performance to date!

This police officer wanted to arrest me so badly. It was like a tall seventeen-year-old girl had killed his wife or something and he had a vendetta against all of us. He searched madly through my purse for anything he could get me with. He found my older sister's ID.

"Who is this?"

"My sister."

"Why do you have it?"

"Because—because I'm not twenty-one!" I sobbed.

He pocketed the ID. And then he pulled out an empty baggie . . . that previously held cocaine. He looked closely at the white residue.

He scoffed angrily. "If there was anything in this you'd be going fucking downtown. Get the fuck off my car."

He was horrible. To him I was the scum of the earth. And I truly felt like it after that interaction.

There was a huge crowd of spectators outside the Starbucks,

staring at me. I wiped my eyes, took a bow, and started my second walk of shame back to the apartment. Mondays, amirite?

That was the last time I ever shoplifted.

The end of summer came quickly after that. Neha and Neesie had to go back to Northwestern, a.k.a. their real lives, and I had to go back to . . . nothing.

We had our suitcases all packed.

"Ready to go, Laura?" asked Neha.

"Yeah, um, one sec." I went out the front door to the street. I stood on the edge of the curb and held my arms open.

"Hello?? Anyone out there that can find a way to keep me here? Anyone want to discover my talent? Please? Anyone want to give me a large sum of money in exchange for my work as an actor so that I can keep this Westwood apartment by myself??"

There was no answer. A few BMWs whizzed by dangerously close to the curb I was standing on. One car honked at me. FINE. I'd go back to Downers Grove and figure out a way to settle here later on, especially now that I REALLY understood how LA worked. Obviously. This was fine!

In the back of my mind, I was a little disappointed in the fact that I wasn't a big star yet. I didn't really blame my drinking or drug habits. I thought I was just having the time of my life.

In reality, though, I had totally lost focus. I had gone from dinky motel-room parties to the coolest clubs in LA, unlimited drugs, and no parents to answer to. It had been a three-month-long party and a high that I did not want to come down from.

When I got home, the questions of how it was came rolling in.

"It was awesome. I auditioned for this huge movie," I said nonchalantly.

"Just one audition?"

Whatever! I wasn't discouraged at all. This felt like a step toward my career. I had gotten out of Downers Grove once, and I was going to again. I didn't know how it was going to happen, but it would. This was just the beginning. I was completely, unwaveringly sure.

Okay WHOEVER keeps calling me delusional, I can hear you and also—SHUT UP.

CHAPTER 4

How to Ignore a
Hundred Red Flags

I got back to Downers Grove expecting things to be the same as when I left. It still looked the same for sure—but all my friends were gone. Maggie was at Northwestern, and Jack was in Wisconsin at St. Norbert. They were all doing great things and making career moves, and I was so happy for them! But for me it sucked.

I did have Colleen, though. She was living at home, working at the restaurant, and going to community college.

"How did my investment do in LA?" she'd ask, referring to all the money she lent me for my summer away.

"I'm gonna get you ten times that money after I make it big."

Colleen and I were opposites in some ways, but the same in others. I was a rebellious, loudmouth weirdo, and she was an introverted, quiet weirdo. She had no friends and would just read books all day and play guitar and sing in French. When we were younger, she loved school and was good at it. She would even offer to write my high school essays for me, scrawling out the entire thing in tiny handwriting on a couple notecards so that I could take them to school and copy them over in my clumsy, boyish handwriting. When she offered the first time, I was stunned.

"Seriously. I'll write your essay for you."

"You'll write my essay . . . and I'll do nothing in return?"

"Yeah. I just love US History."

I took her hand. "I don't understand you at all, but I will gladly take advantage of your weirdly vast knowledge of early-American aviation."

Colleen looked into my eyes. "They dreamed of flying and they *did* it, Laura."

She also had a water bed. Yes, the bed she grew up sleeping on was the sexiest bed of the '90s. I'm not sure how it got that title, seeing how it just felt like sleeping on a weird bladder. We'd slosh around on it for hours, talking and laughing and eating pistachios. And if I jumped onto it hard enough, she would go flying off from the waves I made.

But being at home wasn't easy. I felt my cabin fever coming back. I grew impatient for a way to get back to LA.

Oh. There's one thing I forgot to tell you. The day I got back home, I started getting phone calls to our landline.

"Hello? Laura? It's me!" There was a long pause. "Damon!"

"Who??"

"Damon! We met at the Argyle!"

I had to rack my brain. The Argyle? OHHHHHHHH. Damon. He was the very pretty man I met outside the Argyle in LA who gave me some coke and told me he wanted to shoot me. With a camera.

How could I forget anyone who was generous enough to give me a free bump??

Side note: What kind of confidence did this dude have to start off a phone call with "It's me!" after I had met him just one time, two months ago. As if there were any chance I would just recognize his voice?

"Come out to New York so I can shoot you!" he said excitedly.

I *barely* remembered him. Honestly, he was just evidence that my summer in LA went super well. So of course I said no to his offer! Jeez, who do you think I am??

But then, a few hours later he called back:

"Hey Laura! Come out to New York so I can shoot you!"

"I can't just come out to New York. I've met you once!"

I'm not *that* impulsive. But apparently, he was. He started calling . . . every day. Multiple times a day.

It was always variations of: "I'm in New York, I still want to shoot with you! Come out here!" over and over again.

My family was starting to get annoyed. On one particular day, Damon had called four times, leaving a voice mail each time, as if we needed to be reminded what his call was regarding. My family had just sat down for a formal TV dinner and then . . . RINGGGGGGGG—

My dad, mom, and sisters all glared at me.

Colleen took a bite of corn on the cob. "I wonder who that is?"

My dad grumbled, "No one. Touch. That. Phone."

RRIIIIINNNGGGGG.

We kept eating in silence until my dad got up, picked up the receiver, and yelled, "STOP CALLING, YOU PUNK! . . . mhmmm. Right. Fine."

He hung up the receiver. "Some brand-new, never-heard-before information. Damon wants you to go to New York."

I know what you're thinking. "This dude sounds crazy, Laura! Block his number!" Hey, I hear you loud and clear. But at the time I thought Damon was harmless. It was flattering, really, that he wanted to photograph me! Not a red flag at all.

A few days later, Colleen and I got into a huge fight. I had worn one of her favorite shirts and "covered it with red wine." I replied, completely factually, that her stupid face was the very reason I DRANK the red wine so who's really to blame here. . . .

Now, I have NO IDEA WHY, but our civil, factual conversation turned into a yelling match. It wasn't my fault! A.K.A. it was completely my fault! But suddenly, in the middle of it all, Colleen yelled this:

"I wish you would just leave!"

I clenched my jaw and said, "Well I don't want to be here!"

"You know what?? You should go to New York. Just fucking GO. Just LEAVE."

"Fine!!! I will go! Can I borrow money for a ticket!"

"Yes! Gladly!!"

It took me a second to realize what I had just agreed to. Shit. She bought me a one-way ticket to New York and I said the most menacing "thank you" I could muster up. I packed a bag, including her wine-stained shirt just to salt the wound a little. I guess I was going to New York.

I called Damon back. "Okay, I'm coming. I'll be there in a week."

There was a long pause on the phone . . . until I heard him say . . . "What??"

He really wasn't expecting me to come. Whatever. It was going to be fine!

A week later, I passed my parents on my way out. My mom was reading in the dining room and my dad was sitting in his La-Z-Boy, watching CNN with a clenched fist.

"Bye, Mom, I'm going to New York to be a model."

"Okay honey, have fun!"

My dad chimed in, too. "You're going to kill it; you're gorgeous."

I yelled louder, for my sister to hear. "BYE, EVERYONE. I'M OFF."

She yelled back. "Don't fuck it up!"

I had one suitcase, one plane ticket, forty dollars in my pocket, and a napkin with Damon's address written on it. I was off.

Here's what I DIDN'T have: a cell phone or any kind of plan.

Looking back, I am now fully aware of how dangerous this was. This impulsive girl who hopped over to New York without a second thought is WAY DIFFERENT TODAY. Now, my idea of "dangerous" is binge watching Netflix until two a.m. because I might not get my full eight hours. (Good sleep is better than sex, you guys.)

But eighteen-year-old me was desperate for adventure. Which might just be a nice way of saying batshit crazy. Jury's still out.

When I climbed off the plane at JFK Airport, I was basically a bright-eyed suburban girl hopping off a plane in the big city, carrying a big suitcase and even bigger dreams!

I was ready for my musical number to start. Hello angry people at baggage claim! Hello strange smells where they shouldn't be! Hello homeless person squatting on the curb! The kindness of the city was everywhere! A friendly-looking middle-aged man with an exotic accent approached me, offering to drive me to my destination in his unmarked taxi. Shucks, how lucky am I!

I enthusiastically said yes as I politely asked him to watch my suitcase while I used the restroom. As I was peeing (and probably humming show-tunes to myself), I looked around the bathroom stall. Someone had written SUCK A DICK, GEENA on the wall. I suddenly noticed the traces of piss on the floor, the highly questionable brown smear on the stall door. Oh God, it's disgusting here. Oh God, I let a random man watch my bag. Oh my God, oh my God. I wiped my vag and ran out as fast as I could.

He was still there, bag in hand. Whew. Great! This, of course, was a sign that nothing bad would ever happen to me! I hopped into his unmarked taxi and read the address of my—now wrinkled and torn—napkin, "Twenty-Second and Ninth, please." Damn, I sounded official.

When we arrived, I asked the cabbie if he would let me borrow his cell phone.

I nervously called Damon.

"Hey! I'm outside your apartment."

I anxiously waited in the backseat and looked around the busy street. Was that guy Damon? Nope. Was . . . that guy? It suddenly hit me . . . I didn't remember what the fuck he looked like. He was definitely white. He had black hair. Or wait, was he blond and it was just dark outside? And . . . two eyes, for sure.

A twentysomething-year-old guy with disheveled hair and a beautiful face ran up to the cab, in shock. It was as if HE couldn't believe I'd actually come. And he was wearing . . . bright red lipstick. Umm . . . lipstick? Now I was the one who was shocked.

"Laura!" he said.

He kissed my cheek, getting lipstick all over it. What had I gotten myself into?

We walked up four flights of seemingly never-ending stairs, and he opened the door to the smallest studio apartment I had ever seen. It was smaller than an elementary school bathroom. No furniture. Just a gross twin-size mattress on the floor.

The studio was decorated with wine bottles, ashtrays, and one green light. Which looks VERY MENACING, I MIGHT ADD.

I tried to diffuse my nervousness with a joke. "You okay? You're looking a little . . . GREEN HA-HA!"

"What? No, I'm fine," Damon said with concern.

"I'm talking about the light."

"Oh, no. I'm not sick. It's just the light."

Right. This was going to be rough.

He picked up one of the wine bottles. "Want a drink?"

Oh thank God. Don't mind if I do!

Soon enough, my drunk, naïve, Midwestern ass thought the green light was very, very cool; the apartment was cozy rather than suffocating; and the Frank Sinatra playing on a cassette player was intentionally hip rather than a random thing that Damon found on the street. This place was awesome!

I asked the man for whom I moved to New York why he was wearing lipstick. Maybe he was gay? Maybe the fact that I had no choice but to sleep on the same tiny mattress with a guy I'd met only twice wouldn't be a big deal, because he likes men! Maybe I had nothing to worry about!

He told me he had just come from an abandoned church-turned-nightclub lipstick-launch party. Apparently, Amanda Lepore, a famous transgender model, was launching her new lip line and insisted he try a shade.

Oh, and remember when he said he was a photographer? I now learned that he meant he was a . . . drug sharer . . . who accepted money in exchange for his good will. And he also took pictures occasionally. You might be thinking, "That's another red flag, for sure!" But that only made me like him more because, free drugs! I was getting drunk regularly, smoking weed daily, and dabbling in cocaine; so as an addict, I was attracted to other addicts. Like Damon! He didn't judge me, criticize me, or tell me, "Hey maybe you shouldn't be smoking weed for breakfast." Or, "Do you really need that sixth glass of wine? Your teeth are disturbingly purple." Damon understood my purple teeth.

He also understood my need to numb out any uncomfortable feelings that might have caused slight pain. God forbid I would feel human emotions, right? I didn't actually have the courage to sit through uncomfortable feelings without getting high until I was twenty-four. That's normal, right? And to stay on this track, I made sure to only hang around with other unformed, self-sabotaging delinquents so that there was absolutely no one around that would encourage me to be a fully functioning, productive adult. He was the first on that list, the first full-blown addict that I had gotten close to. And we were sure to enable each other.

Our awkward conversations and public drunkenness soon became love. It didn't really matter if we had much else in common. Bonding over our absolute inability to drink alcohol in moderate proportions was good enough for me.

Within three days of being in New York, Damon was telling me he loved me and I was saying it back. It was love at . . . uh . . . tenth drink.

There was truly never a dull moment during my two-month stay in the Big Apple. Damon would take me to these crazy underground clubs and we'd run around the streets of New York and take pictures and get drunk. And then there were darker moments where I would sit in his green-light apartment while he'd sneak away to handle his business as an, *ahem*, self-employed street pharmacist. We'd pay for everything in cash, and when someone's name was required on any document, we'd use mine instead of his. I began to wonder if there was a warrant out for Damon's arrest, so he couldn't leave a paper trail.

So, just to reassess the situation, I was an addict dependent on drugs and alcohol to feel okay, and I was also dependent on another addict for food and housing. Then things between Damon and me started getting more and more toxic.

I didn't have anything or anyone in the city besides him. When I tried to make friends or meet other people, he would get possessive and furious. We'd often get in these huge alcohol-induced fights after he tried to tell me what to wear or what to do or who to talk to.

"You're too controlling!!" I'd scream.

"You're too out of control!!" he'd scream back.

We were both right. One night, I added to the usual screaming match: "I want to go back home to Chicago!"

He clenched his fists and leaned toward me a bit like he was going to lunge at me. I hadn't seen him so mad before. I got scared and flinched. I think he noticed because he didn't lunge at me. He immediately ran out into the middle of the street, laid down on it like a maniac, and screamed, "I'M NOT MOVING UNTIL YOU KISS ME!"

We were so fucking dramatic. I wanted to assert a bit of power, so I sauntered over to him VERY slowly.

Don't look at me like that! The roads weren't very busy at three a.m. I kissed him and we both got out of the street.

Also just want to point out quickly that my prefrontal cortex, the brain's RATIONAL part, was far from developed, so none of those bad decisions were actually my fault. Doesn't that make you feel so much better about the shitty decisions you made pre-twenty-five? If you're reading this and under twenty-five, remember, it's not your fault. Nothing is ever your fault. If you're reading this and over twenty-five, get your shit together and fix your credit. Seriously, you have no excuse. Right on your birthday, the line is DRAWN.

Damon was getting . . . weird though. To say the least.

His encouragement for me to pursue modeling had started out as just a series of compliments on my appearance, but it was quickly becoming a sort of obsession for him. Like I said, we would go around the city, taking pictures. But he started to become almost manic about getting the right shot. I felt a spike in my confidence at first, wanting to go along with his ideas. The more he told me I could do this as a career, the more I believed in myself. But when I sought out any other photographer to shoot with or get jobs with, Damon would become furious with me.

While I was out one night I met a photographer, Lavan. I loved to shoot with him because he was creative and kind and stable (what a concept!). It was nice to have an actual friend in this city. Lavan and I would go to fancy hotels in the middle of the night and shoot in their lobbies and hallways. I'd wear these long gowns (that I would return immediately to the store) and we'd stay out late, shooting across the city.

When I was with Lavan, I could relax a little. It also finally gave me a chance to call my parents. I still didn't have a cell phone and, a lot of the time, Damon didn't let me use his. He never wanted me calling my family. Yep—some of that sweet, sweet isolation. There were red flags galore.

I'd get home late and again Damon's blue eyes would be bulging out of his head with anger. How dare I betray him? He was convinced I was cheating on him, always. I told him we were just shooting! He was being ridiculous.

I yelled at him, "You know, real models don't get jobs by just shooting with one photographer-slash–drug dealer!! I need to net-work if you want me to get jobs."

If you want me to get jobs. It never occurred to me that I was basically just doing this because he told me to. I still wanted to be an actor. I didn't give a shit about modeling! What the fuck was I doing? But I didn't really have time to soul-search about my choices, because Damon grabbed me by the arm and yanked me toward him.

"You only need me."

Do you hear that? It's a chorus of beautiful angels singing YIIIKKKEEESSSSSS! RUN AWAYYYY! At the time, I couldn't hear them.

He'd grab me so tightly that purple bruises started to show on my biceps. When he saw them, I think he felt bad, because he bought me a cell phone.

Soon after that, he sent me to an agency where he had some connections. He was ready for the rest of the world to see my face, I guess! He thought I was beautiful!!! And also he thought I could make him some money. #romance!

But, you guys, I wasn't doing too hot. I was getting high every day. I had never been so far from my actual dreams and I was working hard to numb my feelings of discouragement. I had completely lost sight of my goals. They were being eclipsed by the ones Damon had for me.

I showed up at the modeling agency. They took one look at me, snapped a Polaroid, and told me they'd be in touch. Okay, I did it. That wasn't hard. You know, modeling auditions were way easier than acting auditions. I didn't have to memorize anything or interpret anything. I didn't have to search the casting director's face for any hope that I did a good job! I could do this! Maybe I *should* do modeling.

As I walked home from the agency, I got a call from Damon. He probably wanted to hear about how it went!

"Laura, the agency called me." He was mad.

"That was fast! Do they want me to come back in for a meeting?"

"Why the fuck did you show up with bruises on your arms and a stain on your shirt?"

I was stunned.

Apparently the agency had called him right after I left, appalled by my appearance, bruises up and down my arms and, yes, a stain on my shirt. (Was this karma for stealing Colleen's shirt??) Wine is hard to get out! I thought that it was normal for meetings to be that short. But really they had just wanted this crazy chick to get the fuck out of their offices without causing a disturbance.

"You gave me the bruises, you fucking asshole!"

"Well you should have chosen a different shirt!"

He hung up. What the FUCK. I was so humiliated. I felt so gross. I walked down Park Avenue, my head hanging low. Then a cracked-out homeless lady sitting on the corner of the street pointed at me and yelled, "You think you're pretty! YOU'RE AN UGLY BITCH!" I mean, her timing was arguably impressive.

I was completely defeated. I crawled back inside Damon's world.

I mean, it kind of makes sense, doesn't it? I had nothing. I felt like nothing because he had taken everything away from me. ALSO I LOVED HIM. Completely unrelated, have you heard of Stockholm syndrome? But no matter how much our spirits are crushed, we keep fighting and longing for more even if it's subconscious. It's human nature. I kept meeting with Lavan, my only friend in the city, to have moments of normalcy, however fleeting.

There was one night that Damon was painting a shitty nude portrait of me as we guzzled wine. We did this a lot, actually. Our tiny studio apartment was covered in weird, off-putting paintings of me. It looked like the den of a serial killer who was plotting to kill me specifically. The green light did not help!

We heard a knock at the door of his dingy fourth-floor apartment. Followed by SOBBING.

"Damon?!" a crying woman yelled out. "Damon, I love you! Open the door! You told me you loved me!" She kept banging on the door while sobbing hysterically. "This is MY apartment too!"

I looked at him wide-eyed and he put his pointer finger over his mouth and mimed for me to be quiet. "*SHHHH!!*"

Wait a second. He was my boyfriend, and this random woman that I had never heard about just said that . . . this was her apartment? What the fuck was going on? Also, I WAS STILL NAKED.

So I did the most obvious thing to do in that situation. Laughed my ass off!

Not because I found this funny, but because I WAS UNCOM-FORTABLE. Also, did I mention that I don't like emotions? Somehow this discomfort was permeating my drunken numbness, which is impressive seeing how my teeth were VERY purple from wine at this point.

The woman outside heard me laugh. She went quiet. I covered my mouth. It was eerie.

Then she started BANGING ON THE DOOR WITH ALL HER MIGHT.

"Damon, I need you! YOU SAID YOU LOVED ME!! DAMONNNN!!!"

Eventually it became silent. Meanwhile, I had put on some goddamn clothes. She had given up and left. When it finally seemed safe to talk again, I asked Damon, "Who the FUCK was that??"

Damon sighed, "My ex-girlfriend, Natalie. She's fucking crazy. She doesn't matter, I swear. I only love you."

Okay, that wasn't what I asked, but okay. Good to know he loves me. I let it go.

Unfortunately, Natalie did not.

Another night came that I had plans to shoot with Lavan. Damon and I got into this huge fight before I left, which was typical, but Damon tried to step it up this time. I was trekking down the four flights of stairs, gown in hand, and he was following me, yelling—

"If you go, then I'm not letting you back in!!"

I should mention that he had never let me have a key to the apartment. I had been in New York for two months by then, and that *whole* time he had to be home to let me in if I went out. And if he was out, I couldn't leave, because I had no way to lock the door behind me. Isn't that soooo cute and relationship-y and not psychotic or frightening at all?

"Fine! Don't let me in! I don't give a fuck. Your apartment's disgusting anyway!"

I made it to the bottom of the stairs, and Lavan was there, waiting to meet me. We were gonna walk around the neighborhood this time, finding some cool walls to shoot against. We might have done really well if Instagram had been around at this time.

Damon barreled over to Lavan. "Stay away from my girl! Stay the fuck away!"

Lavan put his hands up. "Dude. We're just friends. I'd never even touch her."

Okay, *rude*.

As per usual, Damon wasn't in the mood to be reasonable. Or sane. "Just stay away, bro!"

I crossed my arms. "Can you stop being a fucking asshole, Damon? Like, what the fuck!"

Damon looked at me full of rage, grabbed the cell phone out of my hand, and SMASHED it on the concrete.

Great. You know what? I didn't need a phone anyway. Especially not one that he bought for me. I wasn't putting up with this tonight. I started walking away. "Let's go shoot, Lavan. I didn't put on all this makeup for nothing."

Lavan followed and Damon just paced around a bit and fumed like a fucking child. He eventually went back inside.

Lavan and I stayed out late after shooting. I don't think he wanted me to go back; he was really worried. Frankly, I didn't want to go back. I called my parents on his phone, to say hi and hear their voices. I spoke to Colleen for a bit, too, just to see if she was still an aviation-loving asshole.

But I'm telling you, I was so committed to Damon. I knew he was batshit crazy and I was terrified of him, but it was like I was brainwashed. Leaving him didn't feel like an option.

I finally got back to the apartment at around two a.m., climbed up the stairs, and knocked on the door. No answer.

I felt around in my pockets for my phone. Then I remembered Damon had smashed it. FUCK.

No answer, no keys, no phone. Shit.

He must be sleeping. I knocked louder. "Damon!" I yelled, trying to wake him up. "Hello?! Damon?! OPEN THE DOOR, Damon!" Wow, I sounded crazy. I wondered what the neighbors thought, hearing girls scream at Damon's door so frequently in the middle of the night.

Finally, the door opened. Only it wasn't Damon.

It was a slender woman with dark brown hair and a menacing smile. Or maybe it was just a normal smile. That green light really made things look evil.

She glared at me, gripping the door like her nails might puncture the wood. Yep, she was menacing.

"It's not so funny now, is it?"

Apparently she remembered me laughing at her. Under different circumstances, this would be an adorable meet-cute.

"You're Natalie? Damon's ex?" I gasped. I was horrified. What was she doing here? Where was Damon? My second question was quickly answered when Natalie opened the door wider to reveal a half-naked Damon, passed out on the mattress with an empty bottle of vodka next to him.

The blood drained from my face. I felt shaky and numb and every emotion at the same time. He cheated on me with her? He said, he PROMISED, she meant nothing to him.

I muttered, "Just let me pack my things and I'll leave."

"Make it quick," she said in a vengeful tone without skipping a beat. She let me in.

I started to grab my things. She sat down on the mattress next to Damon, cuddled him close and started petting his messy hair while glaring at me, like an evil Bond villain petting his cat. Damon gurgled in his sleep. Ah yes, *there's* the prize we were battling over.

I finished packing my clothes. Then I took one of the naked paintings of me off the wall and stuffed it in my bag as a memory of these wonderful, wonderful two months. I got it most of the way in, but not completely. My crudely rendered tits were hanging out of the top of my suitcase.

I took a breath. My mind was racing as I tried to figure out where I was going to go next.

"Can I just use Damon's phone? I need to find a place to stay."

She just kept glaring at me. I took that as a yes, so I grabbed Damon's phone, stepped into the hallway, and called Lavan in a panic.

"Lavan, I'm in trouble and I need a place to go—can I stay with you? I'm really scared."

"Yes, of course! Are you okay?"

Natalie yelled from the other room, "HURRY THE FUCK UP!"

I lowered my voice. "No, not really. I'm not safe here anymore. I'll see you soon." I hung up.

I went back inside the apartment and handed her the phone. She threw it aside. She was still petting Damon's hair. Everything about this situation was so fucked up. I couldn't handle it. I had to do something, anything, to make it less fucked up—and to hopefully make this deranged, controlling, and dangerous woman not kill me. That would be ideal.

I looked up at her. "I'm sorry I laughed the other night." I really did feel sorry. "I wasn't laughing at you, I just laugh at uncomfortable things. Damon was telling me to shut up, so . . ." I trailed off. I didn't need to ramble at my mortal enemy right now.

She stared at me for a minute, surprised. Her crazy rage softened a bit. She looked down at Damon.

"It's okay," she said. "I know how Damon gets."

We were supposed to be enemies, but I think my apology eased the tension just a bit. I was even a bit relieved that I was finally getting off this rickety roller coaster of a relationship without, like, dying. The craziness was finally over. I was out of Damon's clutches. I felt a weight lifted.

I smiled a bit. "Yeah, he can get crazy, huh?"

She laughed. "Tell me about it!"

Yup, Damon's ex and I were bonding over what a psycho he was as he lay passed out, half-naked between us.

She jumped into a story about him almost jumping off a bridge when she had to go on a trip to see her parents. How sweet and normal! I told her about him lying in the middle of the road, yelling at any friend I made, and smashing my phone earlier today. Oh, Damon! What a goofball.

Our laughter got more and more raucous. So much so that it woke him up.

His eyes popped open and he turned his head slowly from right to left, gradually realizing the severity of his situation. A terrifying, angry, psychotic look washed over his face. He shot up, grabbed Natalie, and started pushing her toward the door. I recognized that grip on her arms—that was going to bruise later. "GET THE FUCK OUT OF HERE! GO!" he yelled.

I quickly stood up and grabbed my suitcase. "DON'T PUSH HER AROUND! I'M LEAVING! NOT HER! ME!"

He shoved me out of the way, then physically pushed Natalie out of the studio apartment. She screamed and resisted as much as she could. "Damon, please! I love you! Please!" But he was stronger, and he wanted her out. He locked the door. I was petrified. She pleaded from behind the door, once again. I wasn't laughing this time.

I was appalled, thinking, *HOW? How could she love someone so cruel?!*

Yet here I was, in the same situation as her.

I grabbed my bag and attempted to leave. He looked at me with such rage in his eyes. It's hard to describe, even, but it made me sick to my stomach. He looked like all the humanity inside him had drained out. He was only anger and adrenaline now. I thought he was going to kill me.

He grabbed me and threw me on the mattress with all his might. I was frozen with fear. He put his hands around my neck and he started crying. He gripped my throat, hard.

"Don't you ever leave me. I love you. I love you," he said while choking me. I didn't move a muscle. I focused on breathing. On staying alive. I knew if I fought back, he would win.

"Okay. I won't. I promise I won't," I said through tears and dwindling breaths. But even with my promises, he didn't let me get up. He didn't let me get up, and then went on to force himself on me. He didn't let me move.

So I didn't move. I didn't want to die. I was afraid that if I resisted in any way, he would end up killing me. It would only be tightening his grip on my neck. I told myself I would get out tomorrow. I would get out tomorrow.

When tomorrow rolled around, he apologized to me. "I'm sorry I invited Natalie over last night. Things got out of hand."

Not the apology I was looking for and . . . excuse me . . . HE invited HER over???

"If you hadn't gone off with Lavan, I wouldn't have invited her over, though. Just don't do that again," he warned.

So . . . it was my fault. What the fuck?

That night, I drank a lot before bed. And as the days passed on, I convinced myself it was a one-time thing. I'm sorry to report that it took me much longer than one day to leave him. The beautiful chorus of angels singing "Yiiiiiiiiiikkkkeeessssss! Get out of there, Lauraaaa!" was getting quieter and quieter in the back of my mind.

Remember how I had called Lavan that night, saying I was in danger and begging for a place to stay? Well of course I never showed up after Damon pushed Natalie out of the apartment. And I didn't have a phone to safely contact him again. Sometimes I laugh, thinking about how worried he must have been. Not because I think it's funny, but because—well you guys know how I deal with uncomfortable situations. While I was off in my own world with Damon again, Lavan was worrying. But we'll come back to that.

Remember how Damon paid for everything in cash? #notsuspiciousatall. Well—and this was an exciting development for me too!—this included apartments. He did not have his name on the lease for the apartment.

The apartment was in Natalie's name.

He obviously didn't want me running into Natalie, who obviously knew where he lived. We'd often stay out for hours and hours, and looking back I wonder if he was just trying to keep up the separation of his two girlfriends that would inevitably collapse.

At this point, Damon hadn't told me outright that Natalie had ownership over the lease. I found out the good ol' hard way.

There was a hard knock at the door. Damon opened the door to see a hulking six-foot-six man standing there, fists clenched. He looked intimidating, like it was his job. Turns out, it was his job! He worked for the landlord.

"You're being evicted."

"We can be quieter!" I exclaimed, thinking it was for sure because of our dramatic AF late-night fights.

The man glared at us. "You are trespassing in Natalie Reeder's apartment. You must leave at once or else face consequences."

I could have sworn I heard his knuckles crack at this point.

Turns out, Damon had convinced this poor girl to put the apartment under her name when they moved in together. And then he kicked her out and moved me in. He was paying the rent, but still. How shitty.

It was in her name, so she kicked us the fuck out. I was scared and frustrated, but part of me was definitely like, *You go, Natalie. Kick us the fuck out of your place!*

I don't blame her at all. I'm surprised she let us live there for HALF a day after the horrific way he treated her. Needless to say, we were now out on the street with three suitcases and nowhere to go.

Damon had a plan, though. We went straight to the airport and took the next flight out to LA, where Damon was from.

Wow, I was finally heading back to LA! Exactly what I wanted! The universe works in mysterious ways. Ultra-mysterious. So mysterious, it possibly makes no fucking sense at all! During the flight over, my acting dreams knocked quietly on the back window of my mind. But unfortunately, it was going to be a bit of time before I started acting again.

From the airport, we went straight to Damon's parents' house in Orange County.

It was a very modest, single-story home in a suburban neighborhood that looked like it hadn't changed since the seventies.

Damon knocked on the front door. I thought it was weird he didn't just . . . enter. I mean, he grew up here. It was his home. Right?

But he looked strange. Smaller. He was shaking a little, and not just like an addict who needed a hit of something. I take that back, actually he did look like he could use a hit of something.

His mother answered the door, smoking a cigarette and brushing her huge blond hair out of her face. She seemed to be clenching on to her youth for dear life with her long pink nails. The first thing she did when she saw Damon was frown as best she could through her Botox. "Oh. So you failed in New York?"

Damon cleared his throat, ignoring this. "This is my girlfriend, Laura."

She smiled this wide, veneer smile. "Pretty."

She leaned in to press her very hard fake boobs against me in a hug. I swear to God I wasn't staring at them, it's just . . . When we hugged, I still felt like I was three feet away from her.

She led us inside.

Damon's dad and little brother were sitting in the living room. His dad looked greasy and mad. And greasy. And did I say mad? I would honestly use more adjectives if I could. When he saw Damon walk in, he only looked angrier.

"I thought you were in New York making money. What happened with that?"

I found out that Damon wasn't an independent rebellious artist-slash–drug dealer. His father had been putting major pressure on him to make money.

His dad stood up and started toward Damon aggressively. I took a step back, but Damon pulled me in between the two of them.

Thanks, dude.

"This is Laura, my girlfriend."

Damon's dad took one look at me and then looked back at Damon. "Bedroom. Now."

Damon glanced at me. It was a look I had never seen from him before. Apologetic? Worried? I couldn't tell at the time. But looking back, I think it was fear.

"Lauren! Come sit." His mother patted the floral couch she was sitting on. She picked up a nail file and started on her pinky.

"It's Laura."

I sat on the couch next to Damon's brother, who was staring into his Nintendo DS, glasses on, knees pulled up to his chest. His body language screamed, *Why am I in this family?*

"Lauren, tell me something."

I nodded. "Sure."

Damon's mother's face contorted in disgust. "Why are you with him? He's no good."

I didn't know what to say. I heard the voices in the other room get louder. Damon and his dad were fighting now. Then I heard a WHAP. Repeatedly. Damon was quiet now.

I was so uncomfortable, way past laughter. I stood up and took a lap around the house. On the wall there were some pictures of Damon as a kid, decked out in snowboarding gear. (Which I'm surprised stayed on the wall at all, seeing how much his mother seemed to loathe him.) When he was a kid, maybe twelve years old, he was a snowboarding prodigy, competing across the country. He was a sweet-looking little kid. It was hard to be mad, looking at him like that.

Damon was not a good person. But in a way, I could finally see why he was the way he was. Why he would be physically and verbally abusive. It all made sense. It didn't make it right or make it okay, but it made sense.

We stayed with his parents for a week. A week of his dad hurting him, his mother asking me in front of him why I would ever be with him, and his little brother trying his hardest to disappear. After a week, we headed to the Beverly Hills apartment that Damon owned. Wait. Excuse me? Why did we stay with his horrible family for AN ENTIRE WEEK if he had an apartment in Beverly Hills??

CHAPTER 5

The Damon Inside

The point of this book is to articulate that people have the capacity to change. As you've seen from my stories, I've been dangerously impulsive, selfish, and erractic. You might be wondering when you were going to see the "change" part happen. The answer is: not yet!

Damon and I had one good week in his tiny, trashy, Beverly Hills apartment. I thought that living in Beverly Hills guaranteed that your apartment wouldn't be a dump, but it turns out that horrible apartments are inevitable when you're with an unsuccessful drug dealer. I didn't mind, though. I was so happy to be back in LA. LA was like freedom to me, and nothing was going to mess that up. I also didn't understand why we ever stayed in that trash dump, tiny New York studio when freaking Beverly Hills was an option! Like, are you kidding me?

Also, I know I promised myself that I would leave him after that night in New York. But I didn't know how. I didn't realize how horrible my situation was, or what a healthy relationship looked like. To me, Damon and I had a great relationship on the days that he wasn't screaming at me. My perception of happiness and love was so warped by now.

We were enabling each other more than ever these days. He would steadily supply my increasing drug habits. Smoking a lot of weed and a bit of cocaine quickly turned into a lot of cocaine and a . . . lot of weed, as well. We'd go out almost every night and meet the most interesting people. Hey! I was networking again. I bypassed the agents and managers with cocaine problems this time, though, and instead met Leo and Andre, two fabulously femme gay partygoers in West Hollywood. They did something or other in entertainment, at least I thought they did. We exchanged numbers. That counts as networking, right?

Life was finally peaceful—UNTIL IT WASN'T.

It was the end of our first week staying at Damon's Beverly Hills apartment. We had smoked a bunch of weed that morning, and lain out to nap on the couch a few hours later. (Weed for breakfast! A great way to start the day.) See? Super peaceful. Until I heard the front door slam open. Hard.

Someone outside had unlocked every lock, but had only gotten the door open three inches because of the chain lock that Damon had "randomly" remembered to put on. How convenient! It's like he almost knew this was going to happen.

"Damon? Let me in!" a high-pitched, angry voice yelled from outside the door.

Damon's eyes popped open. "Oh shit, oh shit—"

In his alarmed flailing, he had accidentally pushed me off the couch. Or maybe it was on purpose. He wasn't the sweetest guy in the world.

I looked at the door and saw one mascara-laden eye peeking in. Of course. Another woman.

"Damon, who is that?? Why does she have a key??" I whispered.

"She's my girlfriend. Laura, you have to run; she's gonna kill you!"

SLAM! The woman outside, whose name I found out was Olivia, was trying to slam the door open with all her might. She saw me, and she was just as mad as I was. Except she probably didn't have the extra bit of terror layered on top of it.

SLAM! The chain lock was quivering against her force. My momentary appreciation for her crazy-strength was cut short by her yelling, "I'm gonna fucking kill you both!"

That was my cue to get out.

"Go go go!" Damon yelled to me.

I ran out the back door as fast as I could, as a screaming match started between them. I looked back at the apartment complex to see my suitcase and belongings being thrown out the window onto the front lawn. I kept running for a couple blocks. Having just woken up, and still reeling from my morning blunt, I was especially disoriented and freaked out. Holy shit.

At least it all made sense now. That was why we hadn't gone straight to the Beverly Hills apartment when we got into LA. That's why we spent a week at Damon's parents' place. Damon had calculated the moment when he thought Olivia would be out of town and took us there, hoping that he would figure it out from there.

As great as this clarity was, it did nothing to save me right then. *Think, Laura, think.* What was I supposed to do? Where was I supposed to go? Lavan had always protected me in New York, but he wasn't here. I didn't know anyone here anymore, but I did have a cell phone. You'll be happy to know that this was one of the fleeting moments in between Damon's cell phone–smashing rages. He had actually gotten me this one as an apology for smashing the last one. Sweet!

Only one problem. The phone was completely new. Even if I had some long-lost contact in LA who could come to my rescue right now, I didn't have their number saved. I didn't have any numbers saved. I pulled it out anyway, hoping someone's name and number would just come to me. And then I saw it. One phone number in my contacts listed as:

LEO AND ANDRE GOOD-TIME BITCHESSSSS

Oh my God. The two guys I met in West Hollywood a few nights ago. We were all super high and drunk at the time . . . they probably didn't remember me at all. No, they definitely didn't remember me at all. I distinctly remember them talking to me sparingly in between making out with each other. But I had no choice. I was shaking and scared. I had no money, no place to go, and no one to help me.

I called them and got an answer on the second ring.

"Hey! Um . . . You probably don't remember me, but this is Laura. We met at that launch party a couple nights ago. I'm really tall and blonde and did a weird impression of Christina Aguilera?"

"Oh yes! Beautiful noodle girl! What up, bitch??"

"Um . . . I kind of got kicked out of my apartment by my boyfriend's . . . other girlfriend. And I kind of think she's going to kill me if I go back there. So I was wondering if I could maybe come over while I figure out where to go."

There was a pause. *Oh no. I asked too much.* I started to blabber on, "I'm sorry, it's really okay—"

"GIRL. We got you, honey. Don't move."

I nearly cried tears of relief.

I stood on that street corner for thirty more minutes until I heard loud EDM music PUMPING from a beat-up twenty-year-old Toyota Camry in broad daylight. There they were, loud enough to be a club on wheels and slowly pulling up on Wilshire, definitely out of place among the BMWs and Porsches that were swerving to speed around them.

Leo manually rolled the passenger-side window down and then yelled, "GET IN, BITCH!"

I hopped in the backseat.

"Where to?" they asked.

First we went back to Damon and HIS GIRLFRIEND's apartment to pick my belongings off the front lawn. Leo and Andre didn't even bat an eye at this. At any of it, I was a random girl they met once. They had no reason in the world to trust me! I could have just killed someone! I could have been running from the law! But they didn't ask questions. They were just generous, and I appreciated it so much. We headed back to their apartment to figure out my next steps.

As I was sitting in their cluttered backseat, I tried to focus my brain in spite of the loud bass literally shaking the seat. I still didn't know what to do, though. There was no way I was going home again. Besides the very important fact that I didn't have money for a plane ticket, I had finally made it back to LA! Leaving would be giving up. I'd live on the street before I left LA again.

Then something magical happened.

We walked into Leo and Andre's West Hollywood apartment.

Their roommate was standing there with her suitcase packed. She was crying and looked surprised to see us, like she was trying to avoid us. She wiped her eyes.

"I'm moving back home to Oklahoma. I can't do it anymore. I can't make it in this city!"

Andre gasped.

Leo put his hands on his hips. "Excuse me? Girl, you did not give me ANY notice. What am I supposed to do? Conjure a roommate out of thin air?"

The roommate sniffled. "I just have to leave. I have to. I'm sorry."

She walked past us and slammed the door.

"I'll move in. Today," I said. "Now. I'll move in now."

They looked at me for a minute. Then Leo raised an eyebrow. "Welcome home, bitch."

I moved right into the other room. It was as simple as that. I slept on the disgusting, stained carpet that night. The room was completely empty except for me and my suitcase.

The only bad news was that things weren't over with Damon yet. He came over and explained the situation.

"Oli and I were together for like eight years, but we're not together anymore. I don't love her like I love you. We just live together, but we're not together anymore. I told her you're my number one. She knows."

Oh cool, that checks out. He also added that he couldn't kick her out or get another apartment because he can't have his name on the lease. It was her name on the apartment. Those tricky paper trail challenges sure required him to have a ton of girlfriends.

He'd come over some nights to sleep over or hang out. And I continued to let him. I kept convincing myself that all the bad things he did to me were one-time things, even when they repeated. I stayed with him.

Living with Leo and Andre did give me breathing room from Damon's crazy mania. I had fun with them and soon fell into an easy rhythm. They were both very immersed in the gay party culture of West Hollywood, so life there was a constant party. I'd come home in the afternoon to find them in my dresses dancing aggressively to Lady Gaga.

"You guys went through my stuff?!"

Leo and Andre looked down.

"Well you both look amazing. Carry on."

They were hard drug users, too, and just like Damon, they didn't judge me for my ways. Quite the opposite, actually. The apartment was always fully stocked with hard drugs. But as much as we enabled one another, we protected and took care of one another. They liked Damon, too, a lot. But in their defense, I don't think they quite knew how crazy he was. They just thought he was a wacky, super-cute bi dude that they both loved to flirt with. We all got on pretty well when Damon wasn't being terrifying.

Outside of partying, dressing fabulously, and doing drugs, I never was entirely sure what Leo and Andre did beyond believing they were in the industry. But somehow they were both incredibly, unapologetically themselves. Even though I was living in constant fear of Damon's episodes, I was happier now that I was living with Leo and Andre.

But then I got a call from my parents.

"Laura . . . Honey . . . Grandma's sick. You need to come home to say good-bye to her."

I told Damon through tears that my grandma was dying and that

I had to leave. Even though he hated letting me out of his sight, he let me go. I mean, what could he do?

I flew home immediately and burst through the front door of my house.

"Where's Grandma? Is she okay? And what's fatally progressive death syndrome?"

My mom sat me down on the couch. "Laura . . ."

"What? What is it? Is she dead? Did she die already?? Oh my God, I never said good-bye!"

"Grandma's fine."

I looked at my mom, stunned. "She . . . pulled through? Even though it's called death syndrome?"

"Sweetie, I made up death syndrome. We just . . . we heard you were in trouble, sweetie. We heard you needed a way out from Damon."

I stood up. "Excuse me? Why did you lie to me? And I don't need a way out from anything. I'm FINE."

"Sweetie, we didn't know how else to help! Your friend Lavan called us in such a panic, we were worried—"

"You don't have to worry about me! I'm an adult, fully capable of making my own decisions." Then I stomped off to my childhood bedroom and slammed the door.

How dare they try to control my life right now! I was happy with Damon. He had changed; he was better now. We had a ton of fun when he wasn't being crazy and I wasn't completely terrified of him.

By "had a ton of fun" I of course mean "did a ton of drugs."

Here's how my parents found out about the whole situation: Remember my photographer friend Lavan? Me neither, apparently! As you might recall, I had called Lavan to basically save me from Damon's clutches when we were in New York . . . and then I never showed up. I didn't have a phone at the time to let him know I was okay, and when I got a new one, I didn't have his number.

Well, it turns out that was very alarming for him. He had no idea what happened to me and he knew the full scope of how scary and dangerous Damon was. He had no way of contacting me, but he had my parents' phone number. I'd often call them on his phone when we would shoot, because of Damon's issue with me having contact with the outside world.

He called my parents and let them know I was in danger, that I needed a way out of an abusive relationship. My parents tried to figure out the most delicate way possible for me to come home. They knew Damon wouldn't let me leave any other way. They were scared he would overhear and hurt me. So they came up with this brilliant, very shitty plan. And as soon as I called them from my new number in Los Angeles, they put their plan into action.

I just felt manipulated and betrayed. It didn't help that I was in this rebellious phase of my life where whatever they wanted me to do, I would do the opposite. I pushed them away and flew straight back to LA.

But first I went to visit my grandma, just to make sure she was okay. She had just finished running a 5K. . . . Just kidding. . . . But she def wasn't dead.

I'm telling you guys, my eighteen-year-old brain was not fully formed at all. Going back to Damon was not a rational choice! But between my lack of understanding at what a healthy relationship looked like and his manipulation and control over me, I went back without question.

I resumed my life in LA at Leo and Andre's house. There, I received two very important things:

1. A slight amount of distance from Damon.
2. The longest amount of time so far that Damon let me have a cell phone without breaking it.

Either I was getting better at living in the complete isolation that he found acceptable, or he had forgotten that I had a phone he could smash. Judging by the fact that he was still screaming at me pretty often, I think he had totally forgotten that I had a phone.

Since I had some alone time, living away from Damon, I could sometimes make calls without worrying about him hearing me. Which meant . . .

Rinnnng rinnnng . . .

Colleen: Hello?

Me: Hey dude. Damon's being fucking crazy again today.

Colleen: Shit. What's he doing?

Me: He just lost it and was screaming at me because I didn't let him into the apartment immediately after he knocked. I was in the shower! Like, what the fuck?

Colleen: Wow. Sounds like that was really your fault, though. Did you have to shower?

Me: Ha-ha, dude! I don't know what to do. I'm scared.

Colleen: Okay, well . . . Do you feel like the side character in the horror movie or the lead? Because the side character dies really early, but the lead usually at least makes it to the end.

Me: Hmmmm. I think I'm still the lead.

Only Colleen could make me laugh about shit this fucked up. We started to talk every day. She'd listen without judging me, or preaching to me, or telling me what to do. So I felt comfortable enough to tell her everything.

I told her about how Damon would lose his mind if I said the wrong thing or talked to anyone on the street. I told her about how he would grab me so hard that I would bruise. About how he thought he owned me. Only she knew the full extent of Damon's bullshit.

One time, Damon was pissed off at me, so he stole my phone. Hey, at least he didn't smash it! He just erased all my contacts and changed the name on my voice mail recording. To Satan.

Everyone who called me heard this: "You have reached the voice mailbox of SATAN."

Colleen and I had a pretty good laugh at that one.

Don't get me wrong, she really was scared for me. She really wanted to get me out of this relationship, and she saw how dangerous Damon was. By this time, I think I was the only person who didn't want me to leave Damon. But Colleen was fucking smart and understood me better than anyone. She knew that if she told me to get the fuck away from that horrible person, then I would probably ice her out or rebel by getting closer to Damon. I wasn't taking anyone's advice.

So my sweet, sweet sister just fucking listened.

I started to get a little bolder with my phone calls. I'd call Colleen to talk while Damon was passed out in the other room. I mean, when Damon passed out, this was not a light nap. This was "Is he dead? I can't tell, but let's wait another hour before calling an ambulance." I could scream into his ear without him waking up, so it was fine.

One time Damon was sleeping in the living room. I was making lunch in the kitchen area while talking to Colleen.

"I don't know, I really think he's losing it. He doesn't seem sane anymore. I feel like he's going to murder me."

Damon's eyes popped open. He turned to me. He had heard everything.

"Oh shit."

His face contorted into a rageful, icy, inhumane glare. His eyes were bulging from their sockets. A vein I never saw before looked like it was about to burst from his neck. In one swift movement, he grabbed a size 11 high-heel boot that Leo had worn out last night and CHUCKED IT AT MY HEAD WITH ALL HIS MIGHT.

What is it about being absolutely insane that makes a person's aim impeccable?

He stood up, fists clenched and head jerking around with rage. I ran out the front door and down the long hallway.

"Oh my God, Colleen, he threw a shoe at me! He threw a shoe at me!"

"Oh God, okay, are you running? Run!!"

"Yeah, yeah I'm running!" I panted.

"Is he following you?"

I turned back to see Damon following behind me in a slow and steady pace. As if he knew that once he got his hands on me, taking me out would be no problem. It was horrifying.

"Yeah."

"Is he running or is it the slow serial-killer walk?"

"Slow serial-killer walk! Slow serial-killer walk!"

"FUCKING RUN!"

I ran out of the apartment complex and hid out for a couple hours at a nearby café until Damon had calmed down. Another day in paradise.

Nothing about my life in LA was sustainable, and things began to get more and more chaotic for me. I started to have trouble eating for a couple reasons. The first was that I was too stressed out when I was with Damon to eat anything. It was like my body was constantly in fight-or-flight mode. Did you guys know that when your body feels like you're in life-threatening danger, it slows down your digestion and pumps your body with adrenaline so that you can survive running for your life for a few extra days or have the strength to lift a car off your baby? That's the truth. I'd be so scared, I'd go days at a time without feeling any hunger. The only times I'd feel like I could eat were when Damon wasn't around. For some reason my body knew I was in danger, but my brain . . . couldn't *quite* place its source!

The second problem was that when Damon wasn't around and I finally felt like I could eat, I didn't have any money to buy food. I was financially dependent on him. Because of my addiction, I was in no state to hold down a job. I'm sure he didn't mind having the control over my life. I'd sometimes be so hungry that I'd go out on the street and find a random stranger, ask them if they wanted to get a bite to eat, and then eat a meal with them just so that I'd have a way to get food.

I never had an eating disorder or anything, but I was losing weight quickly. I looked like I was wasting away.

A few days after the shoe incident, Colleen gave me another call.

"I'm thinking of moving out to LA."

"Really? Since when?"

"Um. Since forever. That was my dream before it was yours."

I scoffed. "I've literally never heard you say that before."

"Okay fine. I just decided yesterday. But come on! Help me get out of Mom and Dad's house. Can I move in with you?"

I think she knew that I wasn't going to be able to leave Damon on my own. I think she thought that if she came, she could help me get out. So that's what she did. She picked up her entire life, quit her job, and moved into Leo and Andre's apartment with me. I mean, she did also want to get out of our parents' house. And LA was not the worst place to do so. We were going to have fun together.

On the day she arrived, she took one look at me and breathed, "Whoa."

I looked down. Did I have something on my shirt? No, it was just my body. I was scary thin, had bruises all up and down my arms, and had dark circles under my eyes. But at least my baggy T-shirt looked sort of shabby-chic, right? No? FINE.

And then . . . Colleen met Damon. Damon hated Colleen because he knew that she was the one opening my eyes to the abuse I was enduring. And Colleen hated Damon because . . . well, you know, everything. But something you need to know about Colleen is that she is very levelheaded. And thinks before she acts. (What a concept!) When she met him, she was not about to jump down his throat. She was strategic.

But so was Damon. He put on his best behavior. Shook her hand and acted civil and everything.

"Why are you so skinny?" she said, pulling my arm out for her to examine.

"I just got really pissed at Damon today and I was upset and I couldn't eat, I don't know."

She raised an eyebrow. "So you lost like twenty pounds from missing just one meal, only today?"

Damon even chimed in, "She just won't eat! I tell her to eat and she doesn't eat. There's something wrong with you, Laura."

"If you wouldn't be such an asshole, then I'd be able to eat!"

I immediately flinched, expecting Damon to come back at me with an even LOUDER, more-aggressive response. . . . But instead I saw a flash across Damon's face that I hadn't seen since we were at his parents' house in Orange County. He looked . . . intimidated by Colleen.

It was such a quietly intense moment. I could almost hear the whistling-standoff music. No one was saying what they were thinking. Except Leo, who walked into the living room right at that moment.

"Can you bitches take your shoes off? Like, what the fuck, the carpet used to be beige and now it is off-beige. Oh my God, are you Colleen? You're beautiful!"

Colleen and Damon maintained threatening eye contact as we all slipped our shoes off.

There weren't any fistfights or yelling matches. Colleen really was kind of brilliant at being tolerant of him, while letting me figure out what I needed for myself. It felt so good to have my sister around. I could finally eat with her, and food is awesome.

Colleen slept in my room with me, on the dirty carpet. I still didn't have a bed. There was one night where we were laying there, and I couldn't fall asleep. I kept tossing and turning. Falling asleep gave me nightmares, and being awake was a nightmare. I just lay there in limbo. I think I woke her up.

"Hey," she whispered to me.

"Oh, sorry. Did I wake you up?"

"No, no . . . " She trailed off. And then said, gently, "You know this isn't good, right? This isn't good."

I was quiet. "I know."

97

A few weeks passed and Colleen remained civil toward Damon. But in her own way, she convinced me that I was strong enough to leave him. I finally felt like I wouldn't be so alone in the world if I didn't have Damon with me. Colleen kind of held her arms open and said, "I'm here, dude. You're not on your own if you leave him."

I mustered up all the courage I had and called Damon. We were sitting in Leo and Andre's living room. I was so nervous. I picked up the phone. Nope, too hard. Let's smoke some weed.

We smoked a blunt. Now I was ready. I called Damon and told him it was over, that I couldn't do this anymore. I think he was stunned, because he didn't say much in response. I'm sure he very much regretted not smashing this cell phone.

For a couple days after, I was just scared. I was scared of what he would do. But I didn't hear from him for one day . . . then two . . . then three. I was safe. I had forgotten what it felt like to feel safe. You guys, feeling safe is awesome. I fully recommend it.

It was finally just me and Colleen living it up in the big city. We were having a blast. We'd go out at night and drink and dance and do whatever the fuck we wanted. I even could talk to random people on the street if I wanted to without getting yelled at!

We had absolutely no money except a bit that Colleen had saved up, but it was all okay. Everything was okay.

A few days after I broke up with Damon, Colleen met a very cheesy model dude. She didn't know he was cheesy yet, although I thought that the bleached tips and shell necklace were an immediate giveaway. Later on, he drove her up Mulholland Drive in a vintage car, blasted Frank Sinatra, pulled her out of the car and said, "Let's DANCE!" To which she responded, "I . . . have to go."

He was the cheesiest kind of cheese. But she was very into him in the beginning, when her view of his bleached tips was blinded by her view of his abs. They were good abs. She started spending the night at his house some nights, leaving me alone in the room.

I said goodnight to Leo and Andre—or rather, I yelled goodnight to them over the Lady Gaga they were pumping, and they incorporated a goodnight wave into their dancing. With the room to myself, I drifted off to sleep. Finally the Lady Gaga had quieted down and Leo and Andre had gone to bed in the other room.

I'm having this great dream. And then all of a sudden I can't breathe. I open my eyes. I'm awake now, but I still can't breathe. I feel this enormous pressure on my body. There's something on my mouth. It's Damon. His hand is over my mouth. He's looming over me. I can't scream. I can't move.

But I'm not asleep.

"Shhhhhhhh."

I tried to move my arms, they were clamped down by Damon's legs. I stared up at him, shaking. He was staring at me with an animal rage. Like he could kill me without a second thought. Like I deserved it. I tried to push him off with my legs and his grip just got tighter. I took short breaths. Just trying to stay alive.

His voice came out in a rageful, shaking whisper. "Why did you leave me? Why did you leave me? Why did you leave me?"

I couldn't speak because his hand was over my mouth. Tears streamed down my face. Don't move. Don't move. Just breathe.

You know what? He asked me a question. I was going to answer. I said my answer through my shaking and sobbing even though it was completely muffled by his hand.

Maybe he was curious about what I said. He moved his hand slightly to hear me. Once he did, I screamed at the top of my lungs.

"HELP ME HELP ME HELP!!!!!"

Damon became enraged again. He quickly covered my mouth.

"WHAT THE FUCK IS GOING ON? GET THE FUCK OFF HER!!!"

Leo and Andre ran in. Andre was full-on wielding a broom for protection. They pulled Damon off me.

Damon scrambled to his feet. It was three against one now. I tried to stand up, still catching my breath.

Leo kept screaming, "GET THE FUCK OUT OF OUR HOUSE! GET THE FUCK OUT!"

Damon tried to take on Leo, but Andre stepped in front of him with the broom and yelled, "I'M CALLING THE POLICE!" Andre pulled out his phone.

That was Damon's kryptonite. I had suspicions that he had been evading the police for years. God knows they had more than enough reasons to lock him up. He backed away, looking angry yet nervous. His face reddened, he was breathing heavily. An animal backed into a corner. He shot one last glare at me as if to say this wasn't over. My blood ran cold.

And then he ran.

I was shaking on the floor. I pulled my knees up to my chest. Shivering.

Leo and Andre asked if I was okay, if I needed anything, if I wanted to sleep in their room, if I . . . if I . . .

I couldn't hear any of it. I couldn't respond. I was reeling.

It happened the one night my sister wasn't there. It's like he knew. It's like he was watching and waiting for the night that she wouldn't be home. I was starting to feel paranoid. There was no trace of him for a while after that, but I couldn't shake the feeling that he was watching me. I felt unsafe everywhere.

But even then, I felt way safer than I did when we were together. Colleen wasn't going to spend the night anywhere else for a while, unless I was coming with her and sleeping in between her and her cheesy boyfriend. Together, we found ways to protect ourselves. I started sleeping with a knife next to me like I used to as a teen. But this time, the knife was not for me, bitches!

If we went out at night, we would leave little traps so that if Damon broke in while we were gone, we would know that he was in the house.

One night, Colleen decided that I needed to blow off some steam. Leo and Andre were out of town, so we were trying to just watch movies in the living room . . . but Colleen was getting cabin fever.

"Let's go out."

"No." Not in a million years, dude!

"I'll buy you two drinks."

"Okay let's go."

We set a new plan in motion. We strategically placed our trash can directly inside of our front door. This way, if he did break in, we would see the trash can moved out of the way and we'd be able to call the police. Genius!

We went out to a club, stayed out way way way too late and got back to the apartment at about four a.m. We both searched for our keys in our purses. She pulled hers out as I pulled out a glass from the bar.

"What the fuck?" she said.

I had drunkenly put one of the glasses at the bar into my purse and carried it home.

Colleen gave me a look. "I thought you don't steal anymore?"

"I'm gonna return it!" I said. "Just open the door!"

"You open it! I'm scared," she replied.

"You've lived more years than me; I'm not ready to die." I pushed her in front of the door.

Colleen sighed and put her key in the door, turned it, and pushed the door open. IT DIDN'T HIT THE TRASH CAN.

"Someone moved it! Someone's been inside," she whispered.

"Oh my God, oh my God, oh my God." I yelled into the pitch-black apartment, "IF YOU'RE IN THERE, DAMON, WE'RE CALLING THE COPS."

Then Colleen flipped the light on.

"Oh . . . my . . . God," she breathed.

I dropped my stolen glass.

The apartment was trashed. Paintings torn off the wall. Plates smashed on the floor. The TV was thrown off its stand.

We stood for a moment, mouths agape. Colleen patted me on the shoulder. "Well, I guess we didn't need to do the trash can thing, huh?"

I started laughing. "Guess not."

In our bedroom, the suitcases had been completely torn through, our clothing had been torn up. Looking around the room, I could feel his rage. I didn't want to think about what would have happened if we had been home. We needed some goddamn new locks, like five of them. What the fuck.

And then we went into the bathroom . . . and found the creepiest part.

Before she moved out to LA, when my phone availability was a bit sporadic, Colleen had written me this long letter saying how worried about me she was, that she wanted to help. It was long and sweet and I kept it throughout all my moves.

Well apparently Damon had found it in my suitcase. He put it in the toilet.

And he pissed on it.

We looked down into the toilet bowl. Just kind of . . . disappointed.

"Aw, man. He pissed on the note."

"Dang."

"At least he put it in the toilet to piss on it. And not in your suitcase."

"Right. That's right. Thanks, Damon."

Sometimes you have to laugh through the most horrendous moments you experience. Or at least, we did. My psychotic ex-boyfriend with major rage issues was stalking me and breaking into my apartment, and now my sister was involved. He knew where we lived. He had easily broken in twice now. I felt like the light at the end of the tunnel was being pulled farther and farther away. If we didn't laugh at how twisted the whole thing was, we wouldn't have made it through.

A few days later I got a phone call. It was an automated voice.

"You are receiving a call from the LA County Jail from— DAMON. To accept this call, press one."

I gasped. Damon was in jail. He was finally locked up. I could have cried tears of relief. I didn't press one to accept the call. I don't even know what he went down for.

After I got the call, it was time to celebrate. Jail time was truly the only way that he would have stopped chasing us. It was either that, or me being dead. I was finally truly free.

I only saw Damon one more time in my life. It was a few years later, when my addiction had spiraled even further out of control. On this particular day, I needed some weed, yo. My usual drug dealers weren't answering their phones, so I texted Damon.

I told my boyfriend at the time that I needed to go pick up weed from my drug dealer ex, to which he replied, "Okay, be back soon!" My then-current boyfriend didn't know how extreme my past with Damon had been.

I walked inside Damon's Beverly Hills apartment. The place was a dump—the result of years of decline. He couldn't handle taking care of it anymore, or of himself. There were empty bottles and cigarette butts everywhere. Paintings and pictures all over the floor. Shadows of what his life used to be.

There was no Olivia anymore. There was nobody except Damon. He was slumped over on the floor in the corner of the living room. There were track marks all over his arms from heroin. He wasn't scary anymore. He almost wasn't a person. Heroin takes the life out of you. He was so weak that he could barely sit up. I didn't feel scared or paranoid—I knew he couldn't hurt me even if he wanted to.

He looked lifeless.

So obviously, I pointed to the heroin and said, "Ooooh, that looks fun. Can I try some?"

He said over and over again, "Don't ever do this. Don't ever do this."

"Just let me try some!"

"I'm not letting you shoot up."

Damon, the terrorizing maniac who manipulated me, isolated me, and assaulted me, THIS TERRIBLE PERSON who never truly cared about my well-being—he wouldn't let me shoot heroin. That's how devastating it is. That's how much it kills you.

I don't think that fact settled in with me at the time. "Then can I at least smoke it?"

I was not learning any lessons on this day, apparently.

"Okay." He handed it to me.

I tried it, but I didn't even like it. I vomited right after. I don't remember feeling good at all. Thank God.

I left that apartment as I had found it, with weed in hand. I left Damon there. I don't even know if he's alive today.

In spite of everything, I don't hate him. He was sick. I saw his parents; I saw where he came from; I saw who he was. It was like the sickness creeped down onto him and overcame him. It's what happened to Leo and Andre. Sometimes I think that's what was happening to me, too.

Years later, when I was sober, I saw Leo in a recovery meeting. He was emaciated, shockingly skinny. He looked like a different person. He spoke about the moment he was brought to his knees. A girl had overdosed and died in his arms. That was the moment where his will to get out of his addiction became stronger than one of the most powerful drugs in existence. I don't know where Andre is today.

Unless you can climb out of it, it doesn't end well.

—

After Damon went to jail, Colleen and I finally got to relax FOR REAL. Things calmed down. In the absence of Damon's chaotic presence, we could see how crazy our current lives really were, especially with Leo and Andre.

Early on, I really loved that nothing ever fazed those two. No matter what I did or what Damon did, it was just another day in the life. When I had called them to come pick me up after meeting them one time, they didn't say, "Wait, what? Who are you?" They just accepted it and came the fuck over to save me. They even loved Damon at first. They probably loved Damon more than I did.

They didn't realize how dangerous he was until the night that he broke in. By then, they were fucking pissed. Damon's pretty face couldn't get him past that with them.

And I think in the same way, I hadn't realized how crazy and out of hand Leo and Andre had gotten until after Damon was gone. I mean, I knew they were using way too many drugs, as was I. But Leo and Andre had taken things a step further, unbeknownst to me.

It was not a normal apartment and that worked for me. We'd party all the time and go out together and have fun. There was always EDM bumping through the walls and drugs sprawled across our dining room table.

One night, they had left some cocaine out on the dining room table.

THANKS GUYS, DON'T MIND IF I DO!

They were so generous! I snorted it and then tried to go on my merry way but . . . My brain went into overdrive. *Fuck. Oh fuckohfuckohfuck—*

What noise was that? Should I try painting? Should I clean my room or should I paint my walls??? I should paint my walls! How come I can't play guitar? I need to play guitar! What can I sell in order to buy a guitar? AM I SWEATY? I'm not sweaty; I'm beautiful. I NEED TO SHOWER RIGHT NOW. THE FUCK?

Then I took a six-hour shower.

The white powder on the table was not cocaine. It was meth.

That night, I stayed up until like seven in the morning. Remember when I said good sleep is better than sex? Well it's also better than meth. #DONTDOMETH

Leo and Andre had gotten into crystal meth at this point, and their meth-head friends were over all the time. Now that our apartment was crystal meth–land, Colleen and I realized that we should probably leave. We needed to start over.

One night out, Colleen and I met Paul, a sweet gay artist who was living in Marilyn Monroe's old house—it was her house when she was still Norma Jean.

"That's kind of like me, right, Colleen? I'm in my Norma Jean phase right now, but eventually I'll reach Marilyn status. Right? Why are you rolling your eyes at me? Hey come back—"

Paul had an extra room that we could move into, and he seemed much less crazy than Leo and Andre. Those were our only two qualifications! Perfect!

We went home and Leo and Andre were sitting in the living room hanging out with their meth-head friends on the couch. Now was the time to let them know.

"Hey guys. Colleen and I are gonna move out."

Andre was on something and feeling it. He squeezed us into a three-way hug. "Oh, my babies. My beautiful babies. I'm gonna fucking miss you."

"Are you touching my butt?"

"I'm going to miss this butt."

One of their very-high-on-meth friends looked at us, very wide eyed.

"YOU GUYS ARE MOVING OUT? OH WOW. DO YOU NEED HELP PACKING? I'LL PACK YOUR STUFF FOR YOU—"

"You'll pack our stuff?"

"I LOVE PACKING STUFF. SO I'D LOVE TO PACK YOUR STUFF FOR YOU. GO HAVE FUN KIDS GO OUT I'LL PACK."

Colleen and I looked at each other. Okay . . . a meth-head wants to pack our stuff. Meth-heads are notorious for stealing shit to fund their habits. She wouldn't do that to us, though!

"That is so nice. Are you sure?" I asked.

"YES YES YES YES YES—"

"Wow, that is so nice! Thank you!" I said as Colleen and I went out.

You know, that Midwestern naïveté dies hard. Even after all the bullshit I had gone through in New York and LA . . . I still trusted people. Hey, don't judge me! It's a beautiful way to live, trusting the world around you, not seeing ulterior motives. At least, until all your shit gets stolen.

Colleen and I went out for the night and came back to our stuff smashed into half-zipped suitcases. Well. A quarter of our stuff smashed into half-zipped suitcases. The rest was gone.

We were going to get the freshest start ever.

CHAPTER 6

A Spoonful of Sugar

Colleen and I moved into a room in Marilyn Monroe's old house with Paul the kind artist, and we tried to get into a new rhythm together. Yes, a junkie had just stolen all of our stuff and we were still reeling from Damon's abuse, but this was our chance to have some peace of mind!

Things did calm down for a while, at least in comparison to what they used to be. And no matter what happened, Colleen and I were together. We kept each other safe.

At the house, Paul started bringing over his new best friend, Adam, who was also Leonardo DiCaprio's completely wild brother. I guess these were the types of famous people we were rubbing shoulders with now. Side note: What kind of parents name one kid Leonardo and the other Adam? Like, I'd have a complex, too, if my sister was named something really cool like Cleopatra and I was just Laura.

Now, remember when my parents had told me that my grandma was dying in order to save me from my abusive relationship with Damon? Well around this time, she really did die. I was pretty skeptical of my parents at first, but after Colleen started crying, I realized it was the truth.

We were devastated. We had to fly home for the funeral. But first we had to get wasted at the Mondrian in order to not deal with our emotions.

While we were back in Chicago with our family, we got a call from Paul.

"Heyyyyy girls. Um. How's it going? How's your grandma?"

"She's dead, Paul."

"Right. I'm sorry. I just wanted to let you know that Adam offered me more money for the room you're staying in. . . . So I'm going to pack up your stuff and rent it out to him. But I'm going to pack your stuff really nicely, though. I'm so sorry, bye!"

"Wait, what??"

Click

He hung up. Fucking Paul. And why was everyone always packing our stuff for us?

We flew back to LA after the funeral with no plan and no place to stay. We got our stuff from Paul's house, neatly packed up in the living room. It *was* very organized, he did a great job with it. He didn't even steal anything! What a guy. Soon enough we were out on the street with no place to go.

We floated around Los Angeles, staying with random people we'd meet while we were out. We slept on a futon at a house with a bunch of frat guys in Long Beach. We met this weird Canadian writer that let us stay in his garden room. We just drifted around.

As chaotic as this was, nothing shitty ever happened to us. We protected each other.

Looking back, it feels insane that we ever did that. Today, I would walk through fire to avoid sleeping over at someone else's house.

After a few weeks on the Canadian writer's couch, he told us that his ex-girlfriend, Cheyenne, was looking for roommates. We met up with her and hit it off immediately. Colleen and I moved right into Cheyenne's extra room and we were soon as close as the three musketeers.

That's when life really started to calm down for us. Turns out having a home where you weren't afraid of being assaulted or having your shit stolen was pretty fucking cool. Cheyenne was this brilliant actress, model, and painter who was so funny and outspoken and smart. She knew her way around the city in a much more legitimate way than I ever had. Soon enough we were going with her to tons of upscale parties and events. I saw her as an inspiration: her career was proof that it could be done. People could move to LA and support themselves with their art.

But then I found out that she had a side hustle. Everyone's gotta have a side hustle, right?

Some people make extra money bartending, or waitressing, or nannying. Cheyenne's side job was to dabble in escorting. How does one *dabble* in escorting? Let me explain! One night she was out at a bar and a woman came up to her and said, "Hello, I'm here with this man, Mr. Peters—" She pointed to an old man sitting in a private booth. He was in probably the most expensive suit ever made, and had one disfigured arm, but the suit was tailored to fit it. The woman continued. "He would like you to sit and have a drink with him."

How weird to have a woman come up and talk to her for him.

Was she his wife? Cheyenne responded, "Oh, no thanks. I'm here with my friends."

The woman pulled out a crisp bill. "He'll give you one hundred dollars."

Cheyenne took the bill. "I guess I was going to have a drink anyway!"

After the drink, the woman came up to Cheyenne again. "He would like to have lunch with you tomorrow. He'll pay five hundred dollars."

"I guess I was going to eat lunch anyway!"

Turns out she was "dating" a sleazy billionaire with sixteen other girlfriends.

Lunch turned into dinner. "Two thousand dollars."

And then: "Mr. Peters would like you to get tested for STDs and spend the night with him. Five thousand dollars."

It kind of just happened. And that's how you dabble in escorting.

She'd come home from a date, and I'd mock her a little. "Hey Cheyenne, how was your date? Did you run into the ten other girls on your way out?"

"Shut the fuck up! Unless you want to give me back that purse I got you."

Touché, Cheyenne. Touché. Cheyenne had gotten so many gifts from Mr. Peters that I got by on her hand-me-downs. He even started paying her rent. He would fly her and her family around wherever they wanted to go. Jewelry. Vacations. Cars. And all she had to do was . . . well, you know! Eventually, she fell in love with an English stuntman who lived upstairs from us. This development compelled her to leave the business.

LA is a town full of rich, old, sleazy dudes that take advantage of beautiful women with dreams. I love LA, but damn. It can be dark here.

Sometimes I couldn't believe she did that. But most of the time I couldn't believe that no rich guys had asked their madams to approach Colleen and me when we were out at night. We were VERY OFFENDED.

But it's fine. At least we got Cheyenne's hand-me-downs.

One night, the three of us went to a huge party at Shane Black's house—he's the director of all the *Lethal Weapon* movies. He has this crazy gaudy mansion that has like six floors, a huge dance floor, and an elevator.

We walked in the front door and were so confused when it seemed empty. We asked someone (his butler?) where the party was, and he answered, "Up the elevator, of course."

Oh, of course.

At this particular party, I saw this man across the room. He was tall and handsome, and he was holding the tiniest black Chihuahua I had ever seen. I had to talk to him. The dog, of course.

I went up to him and introduced myself. His name was Rudolf and he had a slight German accent and a formal, upright demeanor. The man, I mean. The dog's name was Comet.

"This is Comet. He likes to go to parties."

He also had a Germanic knack for describing things with complete, literal accuracy. Later on in our relationship:

Me: How was your flight?

Rudolf: It was efficient.

His favorite joke was:

Rudolf: You know what they say about German sense of humor?

Me: No, what?

Him: It is no laughing matter.

He would then leave the room straight-faced, but I would hear him chuckling from the other room.

At the party, he asked me out on a date. We went out a few nights later, and as I got ready, I suddenly became overcome with nerves. I mean, he was seventeen years older than me. I was eighteen at the time so . . . there was almost a whole ME in between our ages! I assumed this meant that he just knew everything better than I did, that he was just better than me at life.

This is all to say that I simply didn't know what to wear to this date. What do older people wear? Jewelry and stuff? I opened my jewelry box and pulled out every piece of jewelry I had and slipped them all on. Fourteen bracelets and four necklaces. The more bracelets I had on, the older I would look.

When he arrived, I jingle-jangled over to his car and got inside. He saw me and said very matter-of-factly, "That is a lot of bracelets."

I cleared my throat awkwardly. "Thank you."

That was the gist of our relationship. I tried to ignore things, cover things up, and pretend to be something I wasn't. He called things out for what they were. He didn't let anything slide. I loved him very much and I quickly moved in with him.

He was the sweetest man, with a genuinely kind heart. You can imagine how huge of a departure this was from Damon. I think Rudolf could easily see that I was living an immensely chaotic life and he did his best to help me step away from it. He wanted the best for me, and for the first time I had some structure in my life. After my drug-and-alcohol-filled insanity with Damon, I ate up all the structure Rudolf could give me.

For the previous six months in LA, I had gotten so far away from what I had originally come to LA to do. I wanted to act, but I had gotten so distracted. Rudolf helped me focus again. He was against drugs. He loved to have a glass of wine with dinner, but he was in no way an alcoholic like I was. It was amazing to witness.

I slowed down on my partying ways and started getting up early every day. He would swing the curtains open in the morning and pull me out of bed in order to get some morning sun, as he called it.

I would squint angrily at him. "Dude. It's seven a.m."

"You are correct and we are late for the sunrise. Get up, get up, get up!"

"No!"

"We need our ten minutes of vitamin D."

No, I would not do anything for the D. Sorry Rudolf. He literally dragged me out of the house, while I engaged in passive resistance. I was not a morning person at the time. But slowly I started to change. I started to like the stupid early morning sun. It felt kind of . . . good. Damn it.

He taught me how to cook and eat right, and that healthy eating didn't mean binge eating a bunch of carrots after binge eating a bunch of Cheetos. (Orange foods cancel out, right?)

"Go to yoga. It's good for your head." He handed me two dollars. Two dollars? He continued, "Yoga at the Jewish Senior Center is only two dollars. Also, it is wonderful."

So I did it. I took his yoga mat and my two dollars and walked over to Plummer Park in West Hollywood, where I took yoga three times a week with Jewish seniors. Rudolf was right again. I was obsessed with this class and I became one of the regulars with Bending Norma and Angry Mildred. Everyone but me was eighty-five years old.

The only bad thing about this class was that sometimes you'd get there and ask, "Hey, where's Jerome?"

And then everyone in the class would look down sadly. "Oh . . . Yeah. Jerome . . . you know, he had a good life."

Damn, they were dropping like flies. But other than that, these people were amazing. They were doing headstands and handstands and downward dog. They would do it all. I'm actually kind of surprised they let me, a young gentile, in the room.

The instructor at the Jewish Senior Center was an ex-con named Ralph. He was covered in tattoos and had this brash New York accent that cut through the typical soothing yoga effect quite a bit. His teaching method was to bark orders at us. "ALL RIGHT, EVERYONE, WE'RE GETTING IN SHAVASANA, CALM DOWN. CALM DOWN."

He would get into arguments with all the old people, too, especially Betty.

"You know, Ralph, you shouldn't have all those tattoos," she would nag.

"You know what, Betty, there are no judgments in yoga class, so I don't want to hear another word from you!"

"Ralph, don't you talk to me like that. I could be your mother!"

"Well you're not! My mother is dead! Shavasana now!"

One of the ladies there even knitted a little sweater for Comet. It was like I was part of a weird little elderly community. It was the greatest. I just . . . started to feel good. All of these things have since become such important aspects of my sobriety today: eating right, getting up early, doing yoga. I owe it to Rudolf for giving me those tools.

With Rudolf's encouragement, I also started working again.

A model friend insisted I meet her agent, and I agreed—because I had such a great history with it. Might as well take another shot . . .

Today, when people ask me if I've modeled or if I'm a model, I usually respond with, "Oh, I could never. Doing something based completely on my looks just sounds so superficial and shallow. I could never."

Now, this has a grain of truth. I love doing work that I think is meaningful, where I get to be creative. But also it's because I tried modeling when people told me to and it did not work out. For whatever reason, my life is peppered with failed modeling endeavors, bookended with me wondering why I even tried to do something that I don't care about.

When I was fifteen, this model came up to me, stunned by my height and perhaps by my bony elbows. I really don't know. But she told me to go downtown to meet with Wilhelmina in Chicago. I sat down across from Wilhelmina for thirty seconds before she said, "You need to lose ten pounds and grow your eyebrows out."

I distinctly remember thinking, *Oh, fuck this lady. Fuck everything here.*

Admittedly, my eyebrows did need some help. I tweezed a bit too hard that summer. But ten pounds? Asking someone to lose ten pounds who was already very thin was ridiculous. Don't tell anyone to change their physical appearance. I'm more than that, and that's how I grew up. It was always about who we were on the inside.

One of my neighbors was this beautiful, arrogant Israeli model. She would say things like, "You know what is so annoying to me? I am trying to take a bad selfie and I cannot! I just cannot for some reason, it is like I don't have a bad angle. Like I am trying so hard and I cannot."

On this particular day, Rudolf was out of town shooting a movie and I was hanging out by the pool. She had a model friend over and they both saw me and said, "Oh you haaave to be a model; you are fabulous."

I didn't have a lot going on otherwise. So I said sure.

I let her drag me along to different agencies that they had connections to—and I kept getting rejected. For a split second, I wondered if they were just doing a long-form prank on me with the intention of making me feel bad about my appearance. BECAUSE IT WASN'T WORKING. OKAY? IT WASN'T!

Finally, we got to this small agency called Photogenics. The people at Photogenics said to me, "Okay . . . okay . . . we like your look. But we want you to cut your hair off and dye it dark."

I had long blond hair at the time. "Oh . . . kay."

"We're going to send you to our hair stylist and he'll do it all."

"Okay."

"And then we'll do a spec photoshoot and we'll go from there."

"Okay."

So I went along with it. I showed up to the salon and they dyed my hair black, cut it just below my ears and gave me blunt bangs. It wasn't bad! It was a drastic change, but I like to think I pulled it off. We did the photos and I worked all the angles that I saw my Israeli model friend working in her selfies.

Photogenics took a look at the photos . . . and then they said no.

So. At the end of the day there was no modeling agency that wanted me. But saying instead, "Oh I'm a comedienne; I would NEVER model. How could anyone do a job where they're judged solely on their physical appearance?" sounds a lot cooler than the truth.

A week later Rudolf came back from shooting his movie in Germany and was stunned when he saw me.

"Your hair! What did you do?"

"Well . . . this modeling agency cut it off."

"Oh great! So you signed with them."

"No."

Rudolf stared at me and sighed. "Jesus Christ, Laura, I leave you for two weeks and this is what you do."

That was the last time I ever even attempted modeling. Years later I would go on to play models all the time on TV and in movies. One of my favorite characters that I do now is a dumb model. Because I went on all those auditions and shoots, I know all the ridiculous intricacies of the career and industry. Maybe all those failed attempts were like research for my future acting, right? Whatever helps me sleep at night!

One day Rudolf sat me down and asked me what I wanted out of life. What I really, really wanted.

"I want to be an actress."

"Well, where is your agent? What are you doing to achieve that?"

I didn't have an answer. So he pushed me to find one. He helped me get my first commercial agent.

Rudolf was also an actor. A great one. He had this strong jawline and weathered but stern look, but because of his accent he was always cast as the villain. Always. He made a career out of playing terrorists and murderers and coldhearted people who were the complete opposite of who he was.

After getting my first commercial agent, I booked the very first commercial audition I went out for. It was a Spanish cell phone commercial. I couldn't understand a word that was said, but my job was to dance around with a cell phone in my hand. So I fucking nailed that shit.

I actually never saw it, but one of my friends was studying abroad in Spain and called me to tell me she had seen me on TV. Pretty cool.

I mean, I got lucky booking the first audition I ever went on. In an instant, I was making money and became SAG eligible. My first thought was WOW! THIS IS EASY. I would come to realize that making it as an actor was far from easy. But having my foot in the door felt amazing.

Rudolf was this huge positive influence in my life. With his help, I had stopped using hard drugs, stopped partying like I used to, and started to get healthy.

There was really only one bad thing about dating Rudolf. It was Comet's mother.

Rudolf had adopted Comet with his ex-girlfriend as a last-ditch effort to save their relationship, I'm sure. It didn't work, but it did successfully keep her in the picture. After Rudolf and I had moved in together, he told me, "Laura. Today at ten a.m., my ex-girlfriend will be coming over to pick up Comet. She would like to meet you if you are comfortable with that."

This was so weird. I didn't want to meet his ex-girlfriend. I didn't get why I had to. "You do not have to if you do not want to," he repeated. But she wanted to meet me?

"What's her name?" I asked.

"Sugar."

Stop it. Rudolf and Sugar? Were they gonna go save Christmas?

I said yes, partly because I didn't know how to say no to things and partly because I wanted to see if she was prettier than me. I sat on the couch nervously, holding Comet like a hostage.

At ten a.m. she walked in. She was tall, but not as tall as me, with long brown hair and crazy eyes. Her eyes looked like she was trying to move things with her mind at all times.

She walked straight past me.

I hung on to Comet like I was an insecure adoptive mother, prepping him to meet his birth mother. "I raised you! I cared for you when she didn't want you!"

I told myself, *Laura, calm down, this is your house. You live here now. She wanted to meet you. She's going to be nice.*

"Rudolf, dear, make me some tea."

She stalked back into the living room and sat directly across from me, still frozen on the couch. She targeted her crazy eyes at my soul.

"So, Laura. Will I ever get to see what Rudolf sees in you?"

What? I didn't know how to respond to that. I didn't know how to do this! I composed myself and willed myself to answer the question. *Show her who's boss, Laura.*

"Probably not."

Damn it! Not a great answer. She looked smug as she decided I was an idiot.

Rudolf walked in with the tea. I gave him a look that said *spill that fucking tea on her.* Then he handed her the tea. Come on, Rudolf. Whose team are you on?

She sipped some tea, pinky out, ready to jab someone in the eye with all that *class*.

"It's hot," she complained.

"It's tea."

I laughed. Because I laugh when I'm uncomfortable out of my

mind. She glared at me, as if I had just laughed at her funeral and she was deciding the best way to haunt me for the rest of my life.

I clarified, "Tea is supposed to be hot."

She put her cup down.

"Laura, are you accusing me of not knowing what tea is?"

The crazy eyes looked like they were trying to telepathically slam my body against a wall. "Do you THINK I don't know what TEA is?" she repeated.

"I . . ." I looked at Rudolf. He was sweating, speechless, not expecting this to have gone so badly. Poor Rudolf expected the best from both of us. But really, WHO WOULD HAVE EXPECTED that a current girlfriend meeting an ex-girlfriend could have been tense? *millions of hands raise*

"Laura knows you know what tea is, Sugar! It's dried leaves steeped in—" Rudolf stammered.

"I have to go." I stood up. I ran like I always do. I didn't know how to talk to her. I knew how to escape. I went straight to my sister's house. Oh God, Rudolf and Sugar were going to exchange Comet every two weeks.

Two weeks later I was out at a café with my sister. Rudolf called to say that Sugar was coming over to get Comet again, and that I should stay out for thirty more minutes if I didn't want to run into her. I said okay, thanks for letting me know, and hung up the phone.

My sister stared at me. "Let's go."

"Why the hell would we ever do that?"

"I want to meet the bitch who made my sister cry." And she was off walking toward my apartment. I followed her.

We waited on the porch steps, and my anxiety was increasing. I didn't want this. Nope nope nope. Colleen, on the other hand, was psyching herself up like a boxer before a prizefight.

"Can we go, please?"

But it was too late. Sugar stalked up the walkway, glaring at me with the anger of a thousand rich white ladies demanding to speak to the manager.

"Hello, Laura."

I ignored her.

She got louder. "Hello, LAURA——"

Colleen popped up and said "Hi, I'm Colleen," in what I'm sure she imagined to be a very menacing tone. To anyone else, she sounded friendly. Sugar smiled and shook her hand.

"Finally, someone with some class."

Colleen looked at me and used her pants to wipe off the hand Sugar had touched.

Rudolf was walking over to us from his car. When he saw all three of us on the porch, he moved his legs much faster. Sugar broke the silence.

"Rudolf, why did you invite me over when this stupid bitch was here?"

That was IT. NO ONE calls me a stupid bitch except me to myself in the mirror.

"You need to get the fuck out of my apartment now!" I yelled.

Rudolf was sprinting over at this point. She looked at me with her crazy eyes. Classic Sugar. However, she took classic Sugar to another level by hissing:

"I'm gonna break your legs."

What the fuck? I was terrified. I stepped back, and she quickly grabbed my head and yanked out a chunk of my hair. MY HAIR.

She started to wave it back and forth, rhythmically chanting, "I'm gonna make sure you never walk again."

At this point I was screaming, "You're the devil! You're the devil!"

Rudolf finally found his words. Unfortunately, they weren't very good ones. "Sugar, NO. NO, Sugar. You give her back her hair. You cannot do that Sugar, give Laura back her hair."

I swung open the door to the apartment and ran inside. I locked myself in the bathroom. Comet ran inside there with me at the last minute. I glared at him.

"Why did you do this, Comet? Make Sugar go away." Comet just stared at me with his little eyes and then slumped over to the side and licked his asshole.

The messy and unsatisfying epilogue to this story is the following: Two weeks later, Sugar called Rudolf and told him she was going to kill herself, so he had better come over and pick up the dog. She was very unstable. Rudolf rushed over to find Sugar with a knife pressed to her own throat. He called the police, and she went to a mental institution for a while, until she got out and started breaking my car windows every so often.

I never spoke to her directly again because obviously conflict avoidance always helps with everything. Right? *nervous laughter*

I mostly tried not to think about her. But when I did, I wondered what Rudolf ever saw in someone so needy and unstable. Maybe he thought he could help her, kind of like . . . he was trying to help me.

Life eventually settled down again, and when it did, so did Rudolf and I. We got into this lovely, positive . . . stifling rhythm. We got up early. We exercised. Rudolf was close with Colleen and we had these lovely dinner parties that were healthy and fun. Colleen moved into a studio apartment down the street from us. I was getting my career on track because of him. He was so brilliant and sweet and encouraging and everything was right. But it didn't feel right at all.

He wanted kids and a family. He wanted us to start a life together because I was the one for him. But in reality, I didn't know who the fuck I was yet. I was nineteen, for God's sake. He was thirty-seven. I was not having kids yet. The more he pushed for stability, the more I'd pull away. I knew I wanted to break up with him.

Unfortunately, my nineteen-year-old brain didn't know what words to use to break up with someone, or how to say them. So instead I avoided the problem, hoping he would break up with me eventually. My drinking worsened. My drug use worsened. My escapism worsened. As much as we wanted it to, addiction doesn't just go away by ignoring it. As much as he and I both wanted me to just be healthy, I was still an addict. And I was finding ways to hide it from him.

It wasn't a conscious decision, but I knew that the part of me that Rudolf hated the most was the part of me stuck in my addiction. He tried every day to squash that, and he even got me to stop hard drugs. So if I were to amplify that deeply impulsive, unhealthy, toxic Laura . . . he would have no choice but to leave me. Deep down, that horrible part of my brain thought that this was what I deserved.

I would stay out all night, and in the morning Rudolf would be upset, but he would quickly forgive me. He knew something was wrong and he wanted to help, but I felt myself being pulled away by the hand of my addiction.

One night I came home at eight a.m. to him blasting "(You're the) Devil in Disguise" by Elvis. He wasn't even home. He just had it on repeat, loud enough for all the neighbors to hear. I remember thinking this was way more embarrassing than the fact that I was coming home at eight a.m. multiple nights a week.

That was his worst. Rudolf was a sweet, sweet man.

I tried to zero in on a way to break up with him, but I couldn't think of one thing he did wrong. And that's the only way to break up, right? To be deeply betrayed by a horribly toxic person so there's nothing left to salvage between you two?

Since Rudolf was not going to be that person, I would have to step up. What a cross to bear, what a sacrifice. You're welcome, everyone.

I was out one night on Sunset Boulevard and I met an Irish guy. His name was Kevin. Or Devin. We were both very drunk.

"Wanna go to Mexico?" he asked after thirty minutes of talking to me.

"Ummmm. Yeah, I do. Let's go."

I picked him up the next afternoon. In the cold light of day, I tried really hard not to regret everything I'd ever done to lead me to this moment. He had an angry face, with eyebrows that looked perpetually mad. He sighed like everything took way too long for him. He had a weird scar next to his eyebrow that looked like he got a bad piercing, felt self-conscious about looking gay, and then took it out.

Maybe I was projecting a lot of bad things onto him, but also he sucked. He was so condescending. On the way down, he found a bag of ecstasy in my glove compartment and became infuriated.

"Do you KNOW how much trouble we could get in for having this when we cross the border? Do you KNOW we could go to Mexican jail? I'm throwing this out."

Can we ignore for a second the fact that I forgot I had a bag of drugs in my glove box? Kevin was a prick. Of course I would pick the worst guy in the world to trek into another country with. I swerved my car, trying to grab the bag back from him.

"DON'T THROW AWAY DRUGS. DON'T! I'll put them up my vagina if I have to."

He threw them away. I wanted to punch him in the face.

We kept fighting about everything. Where to *actually* turn (MapQuest was not in business, you guys), what music to play on the radio (I wanted hip-hop like a sane adult and he wanted Nine Inch Nails), and whose soda got to be in the cup holder (my car, my drink). There were some red flags.

But I kept driving.

We stopped in San Diego for the night at some seedy motel near the beach. I'd had enough of him at this point. I wasn't trying to get out of my near-marriage so that I could fight like a married couple with this random asshole. Ugh. He got some whiskey for us to drink in the room. It was becoming clear that we both had issues with alcoholism. But as much as I loved to drink, I hated being there with him more.

"I'm taking a walk," I told him.

Kevin didn't answer; he was either swigging some whiskey down or giving me the silent treatment. I slammed the door on my way out.

The beach was cold and dark, so I couldn't even see how beautiful it was or reflect on my life or some shit. It was just pitch-black. I kept walking.

A guy approached me. He was wearing a snapback with a muscle tee and boardshorts. Finally, the San Diego party I wanted.

"Um, hey. Me and my buddies are having some beers in the garage over there. Want to join?"

Okay, let's see here. A strange group of men in a garage . . . at two in the morning . . . near a pitch-black beach . . . with beer. Beer!

"Hell yeah, I do."

He motioned his arm like *SCORE* as he led me over to the two other guys in the garage. That's right, I WAS a score. I deserved to be hanging with guys more fun than fucking Kevin.

I sat down with the two other guys, both of whom were also in muscle tees and boardshorts (come on, guys, the sun went down seven hours ago). Bro #1 handed me a beer.

I sipped it. For the first time, it didn't feel good. It didn't put me at ease. It wasn't strong enough. I drank faster. I grabbed another, gulped it down, not realizing it was empty until I was shaking the bottle over my mouth. I lowered the bottle, embarrassed. I felt the guys looking at me.

I looked around the garage. Zip ties. Pliers. Duct tape. These things are always in garages, right? I'm being paranoid, right? Bro #3 was smiling at me and breathing through his mouth.

What the hell am I doing?

I looked down at my legs. I didn't have pockets. I didn't have a key to my motel room. I didn't have a phone. What the hell was I doing here?

"What time is it?" I asked, feigning genuine curiosity rather than looking for a distraction to GET THE FUCK OUT OF THERE.

"It's just three o'clock, dude-brah," said Bro #1 or #2. The creeping, warm buzz was taking me over and the Bros were meshing together into one Super-bro.

I needed to fight the buzz.

As the world started becoming the round, warm, spinning place that I liked, I smiled at Bro #1, #2, and #3, and slowly placed my bottle next to me on the floor. *No sudden movement. No sudden movement.* Be subtle.

So obviously, I fucking sprang up like a jack in the box and RAN.
Bro #1 ran over to the garage door closer and smashed the button.

The door started rolling shut. FUCK.

My Liam Neeson senses kicked in and I fucking slid under the
door before it closed. I kept running.

One of the Bros slid after me just before the garage door shut.
I prayed it was the mouth breather, because maybe he would keel
over from an asthma attack. Wait, does mouth breathing correlate
with asthma? FOCUS, LAURA!

Something whizzed past my head and shattered on the concrete.
He had hurled his beer bottle, just missing my head. I ran. I ran as
fast as I could. I didn't look back to see if he was there. I didn't think.

I made it back to the motel, so out of breath I could vomit. I was
shaking. I hurriedly pushed the doorknob. Fuck—the key. Kevin had
the only key. I banged on the door with all my might. I screamed.
"OPEN THE DOOR! OPEN THE DOOR NOW!"

No answer. I hit harder, over and over again. My knuckles were
raw, my voice was hoarse. He wasn't answering. *Where the fuck did
he go?*

I leaned against the door, any semblance of hope drained from
my body. *Okay, let's assess the situation.* I looked around. The Bro
chasing me was nowhere to be found: he either gave up or got distracted by something shiny. There was no lobby or receptionist to
talk to. So glad we chose the shittiest motel ever. Fuck.

I looked across the street. There was another motel with the
light on, a receptionist on duty. I wiped my fucking eyes and walked
across the street.

It was a sister motel to the one I was staying at. The receptionist
got out a key, walked across the street, and unlocked my door for me.

There was Kevin, laying on the bed. Pretending to be asleep.

PRETENDING.

TO BE.

ASLEEP.

I yanked him out of bed by the ear and smacked him. I'm sure the motel receptionist backed out of the room, not wanting to have to yet again deal with two alcoholics having a domestic dispute at three a.m.

I told him I wasn't going to Mexico anymore. I was not. I was DONE. I didn't tell him what happened. Kevin claimed he was really sleeping. He said he was sorry. He told me we had to go to Mexico, that it would be fun.

I don't know what part of my brain believed him, but the next day in the morning, we were back in the car, driving to Mexico. Maybe I knew that crossing the border would be crossing the line for Rudolf.

The worst part is that it wasn't even fun.

I know what you're thinking. "Oh, Laura, wasn't the worst part of this every other thing that happened?" NO. The worst part was that it fucking sucked balls and I was with someone I didn't get along with and we fucking threw away my ecstasy.

Kevin might have had fun, I don't even remember. I made my way to a payphone (because this was the 1800s) and called Rudolf. He answered on the first ring and didn't even ask who it was.

"Laura. Where are you?"

"I'm in Mexico."

There was a long pause. We both sounded so tired.

I dropped Kevin off at the airport and had to talk myself out of purchasing a flight to anywhere other than Rudolf's apartment. I went home.

IDIOT

Rudolf opened the door and I got what I wanted.

He told me to leave.

Yay.

———

After that, I did end up booking a flight somewhere else. But it wasn't to some far-off place to escape. I went home to Chicago. My mom had cookies waiting for me. I ate four cookies that I definitely did not deserve.

Years later I found out that Sugar was from a town ten minutes from my own. We grew up next to each other. We probably passed each other at Target, picking up bath towels with our moms. I found out that she had moved home, too, after hitting rock bottom. She committed suicide in the house she grew up in. She was trying to escape, just like me.

Everything felt precarious.

———

I got lunch with my aunt Sheila: my aunt, my godmother, my biggest ally growing up. We went to our favorite Mexican restaurant. When I was little, we'd talk there for hours. She would show up with a cigarette and too much Botox. I would try to swing my backpack onto the back of the chair like she swung down her fur coat. She would tell me that "you're too young for sex, but when you have it, make sure that you achieve equality," as I nodded eagerly.

This time, she sat down across from me, lifted her sunglasses above her expressionless eyebrows, and surveyed me.

"You look like shit. Your hair is a rat's nest."

She gave me a skeptical look and lit a cigarette. The waiter looked at us with disdain.

"Um, Miss——"

"We're on the fucking patio, give it a rest, Charlie," Aunt Sheila snapped, blowing smoke.

The waiter backed away. Aunt Sheila had a real fierceness about her. And honestly, she's been smoking at lunch here for like twenty years. Charlie should know by now to back off.

The best thing about her was that I didn't have to say anything for her to know. I didn't have to tell her about my trip, my fucked up choices, and the way it felt like I wasn't choosing them; how it felt like I couldn't think, how it felt like my body was moving forward without my mind——

"You need help."

She broke my endless chain of thoughts. Damn it, I was just getting to the good part where I contemplate the best way to kill myself. I tried to brush it off.

"Don't worry," I said, "I'm gonna go to the salon later. Maybe get some highlights——"

"Laura."

Damn it, I could avoid everything in my life except her piercing look.

"I know," I said.

It was the first time I'd ever admitted it. My aunt Sheila is the only person in my family to have become sober. She told me what it's like, what AA meetings look like, that it's fucking hard, but if I didn't try I could die. She recounted the stories of when she almost did die.

I promised I would try.

I remember that night, sleeping in my childhood bedroom. My pink flowery wallpaper was peeling off and my mom had moved this infomercial stair climber next to my bed.

But there was one thing that stayed the same: this photo of me, when I was about twelve, swimming underwater. I had it blown up really big because underwater cameras were a big deal at the time.

I was smiling so big, trying to keep my eyes wide open even though chlorine was stinging them like crazy. My arms were above my head, trying to keep me underwater as my body naturally tried to float.

I looked so fucking happy.

I flew back to LA and stayed on my sister's couch. I found an AA meeting to check out at a place called the Log Cabin Community Center.

When I walked in, I saw people laughing. They were happy. What the fuck? I was expecting some depressing-ass dark room like I saw on TV, but this was light. Maybe everyone was high. I sat down with the group in one of their dinky chairs, wishing I was high, too.

My first meeting couldn't go by fast enough. I listened to other people's stories and prayed that I wouldn't have to talk. I wasn't ready. At the end of the meeting we all took one another's hands and did something called the Serenity Prayer. We thanked God. What the fuck? I didn't sign up for church; I just wanted to get sober. I was freaked out.

When the meeting ended, I tried to rush out. But someone walked next to me. A kind-looking woman. She asked me if it was my first time here.

"Yeah. It is."

She stared at me, waiting for me to talk more about myself. What was I supposed to say? That I was a fucking failure? That I was a horrible person that hurts the people around me? That I got high because I couldn't deal with real life? That I was a fucking idiot?

"My name's Laura."

She smiled. "My name's Tricia. What do you do?"

"Um. I'm an actress."

"What have you been in?"

I really just wanted to sit back down. "Um, have you seen any commercials in Spain? I was in a Spanish phone commercial."

"I haven't."

"Great." I walked faster to try to leave her behind. But she kept up.

"I think you're very brave for coming today, Laura."

Brave. I didn't feel brave at all. I felt scared out of my mind. But I suppose bravery is not being unafraid, it's being shit-your-pants-scared-out-of-your-mind and doing the damn thing anyway. I was finally doing it. Sort of. I at least went to the meeting.

I stopped walking for a second and looked at her. "Thank you." She smiled back at me, then went on her own way.

It would be years before I would finally become sustainably sober. It would be a roller coaster of ups and downs. I was trying to do the most difficult thing I'd ever done. My addiction is a fatally progressive disease. It has a voice that used to speak loudly. I work every day to speak louder than it. This was just the beginning of a long road ahead. I wasn't unafraid, but for the first time, I *was* brave.

CHAPTER 7

Look, Mom! I'm on TV!

Colleen's couch was not the most comfortable bed, you guys. It wasn't even a futon. And Colleen's roommate, Rebecca, was not too pleased to see the hot mess that I was sleeping in their living room every night.

Colleen was so generous for letting me stay with her (I mean, it was also her sisterly duty), but I could tell that she was getting a little antsy. We'd come a long way from our couch-surfing days, and she had gotten used to having her own space. I was getting antsy, too! I was back in LA with a whole new mindset now. I was ready to get work as an actor. With a couple AA meetings under my belt, I was drinking and using drugs a lot less than before (it's hard to quit cold turkey, okay? Don't judge me!) and I felt ready to work. The problem was that I was so terrified. What the fuck happened to me? I knew I could act. I used to have this unwavering faith that I was going to make it, but now it was clouded by fear.

135

And now that I didn't have Rudolf . . . or Damon . . . or copious amounts of drugs to distract me . . . I came face-to-face with my goals in a way that I never had before. The time I had always been waiting for was NOW.

I needed to get off Colleen's couch.

I went to Samuel French Bookshop on Sunset Boulevard and found a book that listed all the agents and managers in Los Angeles. I wrote out a cover letter, updated my résumé (not handwritten this time), and got a better headshot. I sent these out ten times a week to almost every name listed in that book, until someone wrote back.

Anyone.

Anyone?

No one?

After weeks of annoying everyone in both the film industry and the postal industry, I got a phone call. It was my mailman, asking that I stop harassing him. JUST KIDDING, IT WAS AN AGENCY! Progressive Artists Agency liked my headshot and was asking to see my reel! They represented Peg fucking Bundy from *Married with Children*! I had made it.

At the time, my reel only consisted of one Spanish cell phone commercial, one experimental student film where I painted my face blue, and one student thesis film where I played a girl who had hit her head on a diving board and was in a COMA for the ENTIRE film. Although my coma face was spot-on, I was not about to send this reel to Progressive Artists.

Side note: There was one scene in the diving board movie where the boyfriend had to pull my lifeless body out of the pool, and I could not stop laughing. Everyone on set was furious with me. After the sixteenth take, the twenty-year-old director looked like he wanted to put me in a real coma. I shall stick to comedy.

Without a reel, the agency asked that I prepare a monologue to come in and perform for them. Okay! I could do that. The blue paint thing didn't let my true talent shine, anyway.

I read monologue after monologue, searching for the one that would show off my comedic abilities, BUT NONE OF THEM WERE FUNNY TO ME.

I was putting a bit too much pressure on myself. It's just . . . this seemed like it was my only shot. And I swear to God, I couldn't find one that felt like . . . me. It did not help at all that so many roles written for women are just plain one-dimensional. It wasn't the way I wanted to present myself. This was a problem. Now, I could drink and ignore it and not show up to my audition, or I could solve the fucking problem.

This time, I decided to solve it. I wrote my own monologue. They wanted to see me do a "professional work" but . . . how would they know if it was professional or not? I wrote a scene that took place on a bus, where I played an eccentric girl talking to strangers. I went into the agency and performed it for two agents, a man and a woman. I had them in the palm of my hand. Laughing exactly when I wanted them to, silent and engaged when I wanted them to be.

"Wow, Laura, that was really good," said the woman.

I felt so relieved, I couldn't stop smiling. Where's my pen? Where do I sign the contract? The agent on the right, a tall man, wiped his eyes. "What play is that from?"

Oh. Uhhhh . . . I hadn't thought of a title. I scanned the room for the answer. Okay there was a couch. Don't call it *Couch*, that's too obvious. The couch was teal. The pillow on the couch is white . . . and those are . . .

Colors.

Both agents looked a bit stumped. "I haven't heard of that. Who is it by?" asked the woman.

It can't be by me, right? That would seem unprofessional, right? Actors don't write. Actors act. "By—by . . . Chris Blum."

Chris Blum was one of my teachers in high school. I sent him an urgent email when I got home. "If anyone ever asks, you wrote a play called *Colors* and it's very good!!"

The agents looked at each other, confused. "Oh! I've never heard of that."

"Oh, it's very new. Very new. New and hot."

Looking back, I'm like, *Damn. That's right, girl. Write your own shit.* I'm proud of myself. But in the moment, I thought they wouldn't have taken me seriously if I had told them the truth. I thought actors were just supposed to act. I thought it was good to stay in my lane.

Original monologue or not, they signed me. #fuckyeah

The first audition they got me was for a pilot presentation.

Now, a pilot presentation is basically a pilot connected to a production company rather than a network. The production company will develop and shoot their own pilot and try to pitch that to networks to sell, rather than the traditional route of developing a script and shooting it through a network. It's a different way to get your TV show made.

It was this hilarious script called *Sex Ed* about a group of weird freshmen college students taking a sexual education course. I auditioned for the role of a dumb model, which I had done a vast amount of research for in my past. Guess all those modeling rejections paid off, because I booked it! Suck it, Wilhelmina.

When I got to set, there was a girl there who was surrounded by people. Her name was Stevie Ryan, and everyone wanted to talk to her. I remember wondering if she was some kind of celebrity I didn't recognize. I talked to her and found out she kind of was.

"Yeah, I make videos on YouTube," she said to me.

"You do what? How?"

This was about ten years ago, in the early days of YouTube. What the fuck was this? I had heard of YouTube before, but I didn't know people were doing things like this. And recording your own character sketches definitely wasn't cool or respected at all at the time. But she didn't care, she was just doing it. It was sort of punk.

I had never seen a comedienne like her before! She was bold and brash and smart. She embraced her femininity in a way that I hadn't ever seen in the comedy world. She was acting and writing and creating shit that was edgy and authentic and original. Not only that, but Stevie and I were at the same management company. We were on the same pilot. It was strange to see someone so similar to me taking such command of her craft in this way. Could I do shit like this?

Ehhhhhhhh, no.

I quickly pushed that thought aside. Stay in your lane, Laura. I never thought in a million years I'd have the courage to do all the things she was doing. To put myself out there like she was. I'll just keep performing other people's words.

Either way, I was now a big fan of hers and we became good friends on the show. It was such an exciting time. My first pilot! My first time working with real directors and producers for a project I actually wanted to do. And I was going to be on TV!

Well, not quite. The show never got picked up.

I was so upset and confused at the time—*What the hell? This was fucking funny shit. Why would it not have gotten picked up?*

I had a lot to learn about the industry, like the fact that your show can be hilarious and still no network will take a chance on it. When you're an actor, you're very much a leaf blowing in the industry winds. Which can be frustrating, but right now it was exciting and amazing. I had loved working on this pilot, and it just served as confirmation that I had chosen the right career. I wanted more of this.

One night, I was alone in Colleen's apartment flipping channels on the TV, and I came across a show on MTV called *Disaster Date*. It was this reality show where guys think they're being set up on a blind date by their friends, but it's really an actress who's assigned to go on this date with them and be their worst nightmare.

Something clicked when I saw it. Hold on a second. I LOVE being people's worst nightmares. I loved fucking shit up in public. This was the job I was training for my entire life. This was just like the time that I ran into the gas station, sobbing, in order to get free cigarettes with Jack. Or the time that my friend Andy Junk and I pretended to be a southern married couple at an open house. When I was younger, during those two nice weeks a year in Chicago when we could actually drive our convertible with the top down, I'd sing at the TOP of my lungs when we'd stop at a red light. My family would get SO embarrassed. It was awesome. See? Being a disaster to the people around me was my area of expertise.

I immediately called my agents and told them I HAD to be on this show.

I sincerely feel that when you know exactly what you want in life, you can get it. If you can be specific and visualize it and fixate on it, it can happen for you. For so many years of my life, I didn't know exactly what I wanted. I just told myself I wanted to be an actor. But I also told myself I wanted to do drugs and get wasted. My visualizations couldn't have worked, because I was focused way too much on using. But now . . . things were a little different. I wasn't completely sober, but I was trying to smoke and drink less, to focus more. And whatever work I was putting in was starting to pay off.

I auditioned and got on *Disaster Date*. TIME TO FUCK SOME SHIT UP!!!

Actually, it was all very controlled. The producers and actors would find out all this information about the "mark" (the guy we were setting up). The mark's friend or family member would tell us everything that annoys him, and I would become a character who could encompass all these things.

"Okay, I have to hate animals AND give out unsolicited life advice? Talk about a multidimensional character!"

On set, we would have a whole restaurant set up, complete with thirty extras lingering around eating dinner.

On the show, we'd see how long before they walked out on the date, and just as they were walking out, I'd say, "WAIT WAIT WAIT! I have one last thing to tell you . . . I'm an actor, those are all actors, those are hidden cameras . . . and you're on MTV's *Disaster Date*!" Usually accompanied by the dramatic removal of my wig.

The mark's friend would run out onto the set, and the two of them would drown each other out in a chorus of "BROOO!!!" and "YOOOO!" and "Brooo, I got you so good!" and "Bro!! You got me!" And then they would hug. It was so fun.

141

As the episodes wore on with *Disaster Date*, I became more and more creative. In one preproduction meeting, the producer and I were chatting about a particular mark who didn't like people who were obsessed with their pets.

The producer tapped his pen, thinking. "So, Laura, we could give you a dog to pet the whole time . . . and then you could let the dog drink water from your cup . . ."

That's cute. But not quite far enough. "Right. Or . . . I could be an Australian primatologist. And I could have a monkey on my shoulder." I whipped out my Australian accent. "It'll be SEW much fun, mate."

The producer let me create my own character! That date was an amazing shitshow, as it was supposed to be. Although there was no money in the budget for a real monkey, so I had to make do by walking on my hands and feet in the restaurant and making ape noises. Hey, I could be my own monkey. It worked just fine.

In *Disaster Date*, I got to be very creative because so much of it was improvised. I played a yoga instructor on one date and twenty minutes in, I was in a headstand in the restaurant.

On another date, I played a life coach named Teresa and I gave the mark the worst life advice possible throughout the date. I told the producer to call me halfway through the date so that I could act like I was giving bad life advice to one of my clients.

The guy was trying to relate to me when he said, "My sister's bothering me a little lately."

I latched on to that. "You gotta cut her off. Just cut her off."

"I mean, all she did was eat my leftovers—"

"You call her up and say—What's her name?"

"Uh, Megan, but—"

I shushed his lips. "You say, Megan? It's over. You are a toxic, toxic, person, who is ruining my life, and I don't need you. I'm never talking to you again. Repeat that after me." I looked deep into his eyes.

"She's my sister, though."

The mark started tapping his fingers on the table with discomfort. I had him right where I wanted. Then my phone rang. Perfect. I answered with such confidence. "Believe and You'll Achieve It Incorporated, this is Laura."

My eyes widened at what I said. *Shit, I called myself Laura!* I was supposed to be Teresa on this date. The mark looked at me, confusion in his eyes. If I fucked this up, the whole episode would be unusable.

I glanced at the mark and continued: "Laura is my middle name. You know I go by that sometimes. But yep this is Teresa Laura." He didn't figure it out. Whew.

I once played a pill popper. (Again, a lifetime of research, paying off! Thanks, addiction!) Throughout the date, I popped Xanax into my mouth over casual conversation. The mark grew more and more worried, bless his heart. After he suggested I slow down, I pulled out a bottle of Adderall and started taking those. Finally I said that I had to "be right back," put on a literal helmet, and pretended to pass out on the dinner table.

He actually freaked out and poured water on me. Which was my cue to do the usual, "that's a hidden camera and that's a hidden camera and these are all actors and YOU'RE ON *DISASTER DATE*!" That guy asked me on a real date afterward—which was a bit odd, as I'm sure I didn't make a great first impression.

I loved the risk of *Disaster Date*. I loved the fact that if I fucked up the hoax, the whole episode would be unusable. I loved the pressure resting on my shoulders. I understood that pressure—I thrived under that pressure. And here, I got to channel my longtime love of thrilling and shocking other people into something controlled and creative and positive. I mean, I wasn't curing cancer or saving children, but this was still positive! (As positive as embarrassing innocent strangers on TV can be.)

I was never mean-spirited on the show. I have never found laughing at the expense of someone else funny, so when the producers would ask me to mock a date's appearance, I would refuse. On this show, I was the idiot. Not them, ME. And I could finally add "making people uncomfortable" to the special skills part of my résumé, after horseback riding.

My dating life had always been disastrous, but now that I was working on *Disaster Date*? It . . . was still pretty bad. Sorry, guys. The show was an awful reflection of my real life, pursuing people that I was 100% wrong for.

I just didn't know how to be alone. I was under the impression that I needed a man to take care of me. Even though I completely, entirely, did not. I was making enough money to afford my own place, and I had friends and a great social life. But I didn't know how to be alone. I thought I needed structure from a relationship, whether it was Damon with his drugs and isolation, or Rudolf with yoga and dinner parties. When I was alone, what the fuck was I even supposed to be doing?

My solution to this crisis was to dig down into my psyche and reflect on where this pattern came from and how I could change it. JUST KIDDING! MY SOLUTION WAS TO FIND SOMEONE ELSE AS SOON AS POSSIBLE.

While out one night, I met an incredibly stoned ex-skateboarder named Brody. PERFECT! We were dancing to the loud club music, drinks in hand, and he said, "Hey, you should *something something*!" I couldn't really hear him.

"WHAT? IT'S LOUD IN HERE," I yelled back at him over the music.

"YOU SHOULD MOVE IN WITH ME."

"OKAY! THANKS, CODY!"

"IT'S BRODY."

"WHAT?"

Soon enough, I was out of Colleen's place and into Cody/ Brody's. Ladies, this is the blueprint for what not to do in your twenties.

Brody was a perfectly nice guy, but he started to bring out my addict tendencies again. You might be wondering whatever happened to the AA meetings I started going to. I stopped. Now that I was a goddamn MTV star, I had everything under control! I did everything in moderation—a bit of weed, some cocaine, some mushrooms. It was all fine! This is possibly what people refer to as "denial." Addiction doesn't let you do moderation. But now that my career was taking off a bit, it was easier to deny the bad things in my life. I was going to try my hardest to have it all.

"Wanna do mushrooms?" Brody asked me one night, pulling a little baggie of dried beige turds out of his pocket.

"Do you just carry those around with you everywhere?"

Brody smiled. "Wallet, keys, phone, 'shrooms."

Hmmm. I had a table read in the morning for *Disaster Date*. But highs generally only last a few hours, right? It would all fade by the morning. The worst that could happen is that I'd have some wild dreams that night. In the moment, I felt proud of myself for even considering the consequences of my decision for a few seconds. I'm so responsible.

"Hand them over, dude."

We were up all night, hallucinating. The walls were melting and so was the floor and SO WAS MY FACE.

"Have you ever thought about, like, pineapples? Like, why are they . . . like that?" Brody said.

I covered my ears. "Don't make my brain explode. I don't want it to explode."

The morning rolled around and I was still full-on tripping. I had thirty minutes until my table read, where all the producers, actors, and director would be present. I didn't know what to do. You know who would give me good advice on this situation? One of my addict friends, Robin. I called her and told her the dilemma. "Do I go to my table read? I'm tripping balls."

"Duuuuuuuuude, this is the age-old question: go to work high and risk your job or don't go to work and risk your job!" I think Robin was also high.

"Dude, you're stressing me out! What do I do? My walls are lava and my houseplants are walking around my apartment." I glared at the potted palm that was currently laughing at me.

"You can definitely go to work. Fucking do it. Make your money, you fucking working woman. I'm so proud of you."

"Okay, I'll do it." The little palm tree was walking toward me. "Hey, stay in your pot!"

"What?" Robin asked.

"Nothing."

I put on some pants and shoes, then said one last good-bye to my plants, "Don't leave the apartment, okay? I love you guys."

"Bye Laura!"

Yep. This was a bad idea.

I somehow got to the table read on time. The producers, writer, and director were all ready to go, sitting at the table. I flinched as I stepped into the room, onto the PINK LIQUID FLOOR. I can't walk on this! I took a step back into the doorway. The writer looked at me, confused. "Hey, Laura."

I waved back, not moving. The wall behind him was a blinding, flashing rainbow. Fuck. I shielded my eyes.

"Come take a seat?"

"Sure sure sure sure."

When I pulled my chair out it yelled, "Don't sit on me!" Oh my God, could anyone else hear that? I sat on it.

Okay. I can do this. A nervous production assistant passed me a script. What a beautiful script. The pages were so white. Wow. I don't think I had ever seen a white this white before. What else have I been missing out on?

"Laura, are you okay?" one of the producers asked me. Turns out I had been tearing up over the whiteness of the paper. It was becoming clear that I needed to get out of there before everyone figured me out. *Okay, I can do this. I just have to be subtle. Be subtle, Laura.*

"I GOTTA GO! I DON'T FEEL GOOD! SORRY! I HAVE TO GO!" There was a long silence as I looked around the room like a deer in headlights. Then I ran out of the room.

Nailed it.

I heard them call after me, "Laura, what? Wait!" But I could not be in there while I was tripping balls! I walked home muttering curses at Robin for encouraging me to do this. This was definitely her fault. Definitely.

Back at home, I lay in bed waiting for the high to pass. The good thing was that any anxiety I might have had about recent events was subverted by the mushrooms. I had a bit of a laugh about it with Brody, knowing in the back of my mind I'd have to deal with the consequences later. Honestly, doing mushrooms is pretty fun. It makes you laugh and see things and have revelations about life. Just . . . don't try to do it at work, kids.

Then my phone rang. It was one of the producers. Damn, the consequences were coming quickly this time around. I cleared my throat, worked up my courage, and answered, "Hello, this is Laura." *Don't fire me, don't fire me, don't fire me—*

"Hey Laura." He didn't sound mad. He sounded . . . apologetic? "I know that you're upset that you didn't get more dates this week." *Um. What?*

The producer continued, "We're going to give you two more. Okay? We just want you to know that you're amazing and we're sorry we upset you. You're getting two more dates: Zack and Daniel."

"Oh my God, is Zack the one who hates bees?"

"Yes he is."

"Oh, damn. That's gonna be a good one."

"It will be. Just please, Laura. Please come back so we can do the table read."

THEY DIDN'T KNOW I WAS HIGH. THEY THOUGHT I WAS BEING A DIVA. I took a deep breath, trying to stay calm and not laugh. I was still high, after all! I put on my most stern voice. "Well thank you. It's about time."

"Will you come back now, Laura?"

"I still can't come back. Sorry. Thank you. Okay, bye."

"Laura—"

I hung up. Wow, I felt powerful.

"Nice job, Laura," my bedside table said.

"Thanks, little table!"

Not only did I get to keep my job, but I somehow got more work from being high? Was I . . . invincible?

Unfortunately, I was not. I did thirty or forty episodes of that show before I became too recognizable to continue. I would sit down on a date and immediately get recognized by the mark. Okay fine, that last part never actually happened, BUT IT VERY WELL COULD HAVE. #lifeontheZlist

Before that happened, the producers had to let me go. I had a great run, though! I would be onto my next project soon enough, I just knew it.

During my time off, I had so much creative energy and I didn't know what to do with it. I had so many ideas. I thought about Stevie's YouTube videos. I wasn't a YouTube star, but I had to put all my ideas SOMEWHERE. I came up with five original characters, wrote monologues for them, videotaped it, and sent it over to my agents. I did this dumb model character and this woman that explodes unexpectedly with repressed anger and then immediately calms down—just little ideas that I had. I expected them to love it! Or at least to respect my ideas, like they did back on *Disaster Date*. Spoiler alert: they didn't. They brushed it aside in a patronizing email. Looking back, I can see that those agents just didn't understand me. But at the time, I thought that this was a sign that I shouldn't create—that I wasn't good enough.

To top it off, a few days later I got another email from my agents. In the gentlest way possible, they told me that now that I wasn't working, I wasn't making them enough money and they had to fire me. They added a friendly notice that I could pick up my things in the front lobby with the security guard. They weren't the greatest ever.

I picked up my headshots from the security guard and walked home, so bummed. I won't lie and say this didn't sting—it did, A LOT—but I was immediately desperate to find more work. Nothing was going to stop me from acting. So when I met a very loud, frumpy manager at the *Disaster Date* wrap party, I quickly agreed to let him manage me.

"Please, PLEASE, let me manage you, Laura. I can get you some jobs! I swear to God I can!"

Um . . . If I didn't have doubts before, I did after that pitch. But what did I have to lose? He was as desperate for clients as I was for work. And . . . he actually saw something in me. At least he would be less likely to fire me like Progressive Artists did. I quickly signed with him. His name was David Rosenberg, he lived in a studio apartment with his mother, and what he had going on was this: NOT MUCH.

He would call me and offer me auditions for the worst roles ever. "Laura, I need you to go to this audition. I know it's a small role, but there's no such thing as a small role! Only small actors! And you're very tall!"

"David. You're losing me."

"If you don't book this part there's a chance I will starve to death and it will be partially your fault."

Jesus, David.

Coming off *Disaster Date*, where I was given so much creative freedom and respect, it was strange to go back to completely scripted characters, especially ones who had almost no lines. Also, my ego had inflated a bit. Sorry, but come on! I was *leading* those episodes of *Disaster Date*! And now I was supposed to beg casting directors to let me be a glorified extra? No thank you.

But then David begged. "PLEASE, LAURA, I GOTTA PAY MY RENT. SO IF YOU COULD BOOK IT, IT WOULD BE GREAT. My mother and I thank you!"

Oh my God, fine.

David sent me on an audition for a co-star role on a TV sitcom called *'Til Death* on FOX. It was for the role of the daughter's stoner best friend. Co-star was a bit of an exaggeration—it was three lines. But you know what? I was going to make the most of it. I could *nail* a stoner girl character. More of my life's training was becoming useful! I went in for the audition and killed it. With my three lines I had all the producers there laughing out loud. David later informed me that I'd booked the role:

"YAY I CAN EAT! THANKS, LAURA!"

"No problem, David."

'Til Death starred Brad Garrett, JB Smoove, and Joely Fisher. It had a great cast with amazing comedians and great writers. But . . . for some reason, this sitcom put the "shit" in shitshow. It also put the "show" in shitshow. It was just a . . . shitshow. It was no one's fault, really. Sometimes the magic just isn't there. The producers were always in a state of emergency trying to revive the show with new actors, new writers, new everything. I came on in the second season, where the actress who previously played the daughter was being replaced, and her best friend was being randomly added in. They were hoping these changes would help ratings.

When I stepped on set for rehearsal for the first time, my bruised ego over being a glorified extra quickly faded away. I was on a real-life network sitcom! I was on a real set! There was a live audience! We were shooting in three days! This. Was. Incredible! We had our first table read with the entire cast, and I loved it. Again, I made everyone laugh with my three lines. Brad Garrett laughed! It was incredible. How the fuck was this my life?

While I was there I wanted to soak up every bit of information that I possibly could. I watched the actress playing the daughter rehearse the dining room scene on set with Brad Garrett and Joely Fisher. I watched what she did, how she took her mark and went for the laughs. Eh, I would have done a few things differently. I would have emphasized a few different words. I looked down at the script as I watched her and noticed she missed a few jokes here and there. Did she not understand the script? Also, she didn't look like Brad Garrett at all. He is a giant, and she was like five feet. I shrugged: fine, it wasn't my place to judge.

I hopped down from the studio audience seats and I was approached by the casting director.

"Laura. We want you to read for the role of the daughter. The network was not happy with the current daughter's table read."

WHAT? Wait. Wait. WHAT???? The daughter role is HUGE. It's a series regular role! It's a mile above the stoner best friend. This is the type of role that opens doors for an actor. I blurted out, "Is it because I'm tall?"

"Um, no. We just loved you. But your height does work well with Brad's. Here's the script. Take a look at scene two and you're going to read for it in fifteen minutes."

Holy fucking shit. I took the script from her with shaking hands. *Be cool, Laura.* "No problemo."

"Sorry?"

"Nothing! Thanks!"

I opened the script and took a look at the scene I was supposed to fucking memorize in fifteen minutes. When I read the page, I put the script down and said a silent thank-you to the universe. It was the scene I had just been studying. The one that Brad and the daughter were doing a short while ago on the stage. I knew this scene already!

Fifteen minutes later, I stepped onto the stage with Brad and Joely, in front of twenty angry-looking executives from the network and production company. They were probably stressed out of their minds about the fact that they were shooting a live sitcom in three days and had no clue who would fill one of the major roles. *Ummm, can anyone get out here and warm up the crowd? No? All right.*

I could tell that none of them thought that I, this random, lanky nobody, was going to be the answer to their problems. Yeah, I did my three lines well, but this role was huge. How was I supposed to hold it up? I was NOBODY to them.

We started the scene. I didn't make the rookie mistake of looking directly at any of the executives this time, but a minute or so in, I started to hear some laughs. I started to feel the room lighten. I felt their relief. The laughs got louder. I WAS KILLING IT. Holy fuck! Twenty minutes later, the casting director told me that I got the role.

When David found out, he was as happy as Larry. (Also, who the fuck is Larry and why is he so damn happy?)

"HOLY SHIT, LAURA, I KNEW IT! I KNEW YOU WERE A STAR! I'M TAKING YOU TO THE OLIVE GARDEN TO CELEBRATE!"

And that's how I went from being a side character to being a series regular in one day. It was an insane mix of random preparedness and lightning in a bottle and doing my job like I always knew I could.

It was crazy, man. It's the kind of Hollywood story that you hear about but you never believe actually happens. After that, shit got even crazier.

We shot the first episode on the Sony lot in front of a live audience and it went incredibly well. I was on a high. I drove off the lot afterward and this black Range Rover rolls up next to my car. The window rolled down and this bigshot woman in a fucking suit whipped off her sunglasses and leaned out the window a bit. "Excuse me!" she yelled.

I rolled down my window, confused.

"Did I take your parking spot? Sorry, I'm leaving now!" I put my car in reverse.

"Don't leave, you amazing idiot! I'm Lindsay Howard, an agent at APA. We love your work and we want to represent you. Take my card." She threw her business card into my car and it landed in my lap. Even her aim was badass. APA is one of the largest agencies in the US. Holy shit!

It was an incredible time. Every big agency was calling me up, trying to make money off my success. They were wining and dining me, and it felt great!

The best part was the call I got from my old agents at Progressive Artists, the assholes who fired me over email. "Laura, we just wanted to say that we made a terrible mistake. We would love to have you back."

"You know, that is so sweet. I actually have meetings lined up with Gersh, APA, and WME, but if none of those work out, I'll call you, okay?"

It was the sweetest revenge.

Out of all of those agencies, I knew I wanted to be signed with APA. They specialized in comedy, and I could feel that it was right. David and I went to meet with Lindsay, the agent at APA, and it was the first meeting I had where I had no reason to feel nervous at all. For the first time, the agency wanted *me*. I didn't have to beg or try to change myself to be what they wanted. I was a moneymaker to them and I was ready to utilize my power. I had a list of demands ready.

"I want to be signed literary AND theatrical. I'm a creator. I want to do it all." It was the first time I had ever said it out loud.

Lindsay wrote this down. "Sure sure sure! I just need to see your writing, but we can make that happen for you."

I shook her hand confidently. "I will send something over in the next couple days."

I quickly realized what I had just signed up for. They needed to see my writing? Um, I should write something, then. I went home that night, took out my laptop, and wrote. For the first time, I just wrote. I didn't think or judge myself or have any idea of what the fuck I was doing or where it was going, but I did it. I ended up with this dark comedy based on my relationship with Rudolf. I wrote it in a Word doc and tried to manually mimic script formatting rather than getting Final Draft script software. It looked like absolute shit. But I sent it over to Lindsay, and we met the next day.

In her high-rise office, she looked at me over her glasses. "The grammar is godawful. Your spelling is illegible. And get Final Draft for God's sake, I could barely look at the formatting on these pages. But, this is one of the funniest scripts I've ever read."

Just like that, I got my literary agent. I had always been a creator, one way or another. But now, I finally felt like one. I felt all these ideas coming to me. It was incredible.

I told my agent that I had a great idea for a feature and she told me to bring in the script. Again I went home to write it. But, you guys, features are really fucking long. Scripts are usually a minute per page, and when you think of writing a movie, which usually lasts 90–120 minutes . . . that's a lot of pages. My agents can't wait that long! I decided to just bring in the first three pages. I'd reel them in and then make them wait a little.

I brought the three pages in, read through it with them, and had my agents laughing their asses off. They wanted to see the rest. Great! Now all I had to do . . . was write it and not fuck it up. And get the structure right. And not spell anything wrong. And not be a fucking failure. And not come up with a pile of trash. I stared at my computer screen for three hours without writing a word. More doubt and fear was creeping into my head by the minute. I couldn't write, why did I ever think I could? I was so disappointed in myself. I got a glass, poured myself a shot of vodka, and slammed it down.

Days passed, then weeks. The weight of this script was bearing down on me. I knew by now my agents had completely forgotten about it. There was no point in finishing it. Whatever. I wasn't a writer, anyway.

These were all the things I told myself so I wouldn't have to walk through my fear of failure. The voice in my head telling me to create and the voice in my head telling me I was a piece of shit were in an all-out battle.

I started to drink and use more, in an effort to drown out both of them. I wanted to be in a steady, unfeeling, neutral state! That's healthy, right?

I kept up appearances at work for the most part, because I still took that job so seriously, but my lack of a creative outlet made me . . . a worse person. Especially to Brody. I became clingy. Failing to derive my life's meaning from creating, I looked to Brody for meaning. You guys, no one should be searching for meaning in a guy named Brody. Unless you are a guy named Brody—then by all means, search within yourself.

My clinginess and neediness became all too much for Brody. He could tell that this wasn't a good relationship and we weren't right for each other. So he dumped me. And honestly, how DARE he?

"Just go, Laura. Just be independent," he sighed to me from across the dining room table.

Excuse me?! I WAS independent. I had a job on a sitcom! I knew how to be on my own . . . I just didn't want to be! It was MY choice to jump from one man to the next. Right?

Okay fine. Ugh, Brody was right—I was so afraid of being on my own. Even in the months that I was single, I had either Leo, Andre, or Colleen looking after me. I had never been independent before. I had no idea how to be.

Looking back, being dumped was the best thing that ever could have happened to me. I should call up Brody and thank that dude. And possibly apologize for what I did next.

Then-Laura did not share current-Laura's grateful attitude. Then-Laura was filled with rage and pulled a Damon: I trashed his apartment. I threw everything off our (or . . . his, I guess) dining room table. I pulled a framed painting off the wall and smashed it on the ground. Glass shattered everywhere.

Brody watched me trash his house, quietly interjecting "Duuuude" and "Bro, stop it" a few times. But mostly he didn't do anything. Finally I tired myself out and paused, breathing heavily.

"Just leave, Laura."

I grabbed my stuff and left. *What the fuck am I supposed to do?* I thought I was incapable of being on my own.

It turns out, I wasn't. I had enough money from the show to get my own place.

For the first time, I moved into an apartment by myself. You know what? Living alone is awesome! I went from wearing pants some of the time to wearing pants none of the time. We don't need pants! (Unless it's cold, or your couch is made of leather.)

I threw myself into decorating my place. I had a great job, and things were good. My life had always been chaotic. And now, suddenly, it was peaceful.

Thanks, Brody!

———

'Til Death, a total shitshow, but MY total shitshow, was not doing well. The ratings were low and though they didn't express their doubt to us, executives had no idea how to fix it. So their solution was to fire everyone possible. They got rid of JB Smoove, all twenty-three writers, the showrunner, and me. They actually did this pretty often, both before and after my stint. The show had a ridiculously high turnover rate. Over the course of four seasons, *'Til Death* had four different women play the daughter character, not including the girl who did the table read and got fired immediately. The script completely ignored this fact. First it was Krysten Ritter, then me, then Lindsey Broad, then Kate Micucci.

Honestly, I don't know why they thought firing any of us would fix the show. These women are all amazing actresses and comediennes.

I could easily justify being fired. I mean, they fired everyone! It wasn't my fault. I hadn't done a bad job. We were all just dealt a poor hand. But in the back of my mind . . . the very, very farthest back corners of it . . . I couldn't help but wonder if my addiction had anything to do with it. I hid it very well from everyone and never let it hinder my work, but I had the sneaking suspicion that people could tell I was an addict. I used to bring Brody to set sometimes, and he was not, by any means, hiding his drug use from the public. Brad Garrett wasn't a huge fan of him. I remember showing up to work late once because I was so sick from drinking all night. When I walked in, I just had this horrible feeling that everyone knew. Brad asked with a smug smile, "Where's skater boy?"

Brody was a good guy, but everyone could see that we were up to no good together.

I tried to brush off the doubt, but I wondered if I would have been one of the people asked to stay if I . . . wasn't caught up in my addiction.

After I got fired from *'Til Death*, my agents at APA fired me as well. When it rains, it pours! It was the same deal as when I got fired from Progressive Artists: I wasn't making them enough money anymore, so I was useless to them. I was never a real person to them, I was a commodity. I never took my chance to write them that feature. I wondered if they might have kept me if I had finished it instead of drinking.

Desperate for more work, I reached out to all the agencies that previously wanted me. I called WILLIAM MORRIS. "Heyyyyy, remember when you guys said to reach out if I needed anything? Well if you're still accepting new clients, I'd love to meet . . . Hello?"

They ghosted me. Pretty sure all those agencies started screening my calls.

WHAT THE HELL, PEOPLE?

I always had this unwavering faith that I was going to make it . . . but I was finally starting to see some cracks in that faith. Light was shining through puncture holes . . . and I was going to have to do something about them. I couldn't ignore my addiction anymore.

CHAPTER 8

New Beginnings
(But, like, for real)

Sometimes it's hard to figure out when you have a problem. There's a very thin line between doing something you find enjoyable and destroying your life. It's thin, people!

For example: hoarding. Sometimes you just want to hold on to your childhood blankie AND the locket you got at your baptism AND all the empty yogurt containers that you've ever used. And then *all of a sudden* you need an intervention. It was the same with me. Sometimes I just wanted to get a little high and drink a little, then do some cocaine, except things got fuzzy and my life was destroyed. How was I supposed to know that it was a problem?

I could count all the times that I thought I was going to die from a drinking- or drug-related issue on . . . two hands and one foot. My aunt had told me I had a problem, Colleen had told me I had a problem, a random stranger at a NIGHTCLUB (where presumably everyone was drinking) told me I had a problem. It was that obvious, guys, but *who knew* if I really needed to change? Honestly, I was twenty-three years old! Wasn't I supposed to be going out every night and getting fucked up at this age? Wasn't I supposed to be in my "party phase"? I thought I was fine. Even after starting to attend AA meetings, I still didn't stop using. I would go and listen to other people's stories, hearing some that were eerily similar to mine, but did I really have to change? I thought I was balancing everything well. I was booking jobs and auditioning every day. I was a working actor, able to support myself without a side hustle. I was dating and enjoying that sweet independence I got after being dumped. Things were going great.

I had a great group of friends, and I was hiding my addiction well from all of them. None of them knew I had a problem; they thought I knew how to have a good time!

But then I started to become more aware as the consequences crept up to me. I didn't have a typical "come to Jesus" moment as many other sober people describe. It was as if I started watching myself from afar. Laura-from-afar started judging me. I would go to an AA meeting and then pick up a bottle of wine on the way home. What the fuck are you doing, Laura?

Then, I started buying cocaine during the day. This was a bad sign. You guys, picking up cocaine should not be on your to-do list. When you're choosing your grocery store and dry cleaner because they're on the way to your drug dealer's spot, you have a problem.

I suddenly realized everything was escalating. I couldn't drink without buying drugs, and I couldn't do either of them without getting to the point where I didn't care if I woke up the next day. I had no control over this. Any semblance of balance I had in my life was totally false. I was completely at the whim of my addiction. I still had the first three pages of that feature script back at home taunting me, because I was always too high to work on it. How did getting high become more important than my career?

Throughout my time in LA, I had still been keeping in touch with my old friends from home. Jack was still my best friend, even if we only talked over the phone and online. He was one of the only people who knew I had a problem and encouraged me to fix it. And just as I reached my breaking point with my addiction, Jack's boyfriend committed suicide. He was devastated. We both needed each other.

During one of our phone calls I had an idea. "Move to LA with me. Let's start over together."

"Are you serious?"

"Why the fuck not, dude? There's no snow here. People wear shorts in winter."

There was a pause. I held my breath. I heard Jack sniffle. "I do have a lot of shorts that need wearing."

And just like that, Jack moved to LA to start a new life. With him near me, I tried to do the same.

It's weird—I had realized I had a problem over and over again in the past, but this was the first time that I felt truly strong enough to be sober. Maybe it was having Jack around and Colleen nearby. Maybe it was the impending auditions I had to go on. Maybe it was my independence. Maybe it was all the AA meetings I had attended, accumulating in the back of my mind—all the people I had watched become sober and successful. Whatever it was, I could really see that my addiction was getting in the way of my goals. I was finally ready to change.

I walked to the Log Cabin Community Center, where my AA

meetings were held, and stood outside for a moment. I could still go back home and light up . . . literally anything. I'd smoke lawn clippings at this point if it could numb my dread. Unfortunately, California was in a drought and there were only succulents around.

There were, however, about fifty twentysomething, punk-looking kids covered in tattoos, sitting around outside, smoking cigarettes. I had seen them before when I had gone to meetings, but never really took notice of them. They were laughing . . . and bright eyed. They looked clear and happy. Is this what sobriety looks like? Nah, they must be high!

I must have been staring for too long, because this badass-looking, tattooed girl came over to me. She did a grand gesture with her arms.

"Welcome."

"Thanks," I muttered, but I didn't move.

"Are you going in?" she continued.

I hesistated. I wanted to get sober, of course, but I had been to meetings before. I knew that when I went inside, they would ask us to turn ourselves over to God, and then I would immediately check out like I had always done.

I could still hear my dad's voice in the back of my head: "FUCK ORGANIZED RELIGION! It's bullshit. And eat another hot dog, Laura, you're too skinny!"

There was no way I'd believe any of this. *Okay, bye!!!* Yet there was something about this tatted woman's kind face. I told her everything on my mind. She just smiled at me.

"No, no, we're not a religious program. God can be any higher power of your own understanding. It could be the sun or mother nature. It can be anything."

"Penguins?"

"If you want."

Okay, well, I am deeply fond of penguins.

I took a deep breath and walked inside. And from there . . . I just did it. I was ready and open. I got on my knees and turned myself over to the penguins or whoever the fuck was looking out for me.

I started to learn things that changed my life. I badly needed to find happiness, to let go of whatever horrible feelings about myself that I felt the urge to numb and ignore.

The first thing I learned was the Serenity Prayer:

God, grant me the serenity
To accept the things I cannot change;
Courage to change the things I can;
And wisdom to know the difference.

It sounds so simple, but it was huge for me. If I was unhappy with a situation, I either needed to truly accept it or—if possible—to work through my fear in order to change it. I started to apply this to my acting. If I was unhappy with the work I was getting or the lack thereof, I couldn't drink and ignore it. I needed to have the courage to change the things I can by putting myself out there in a different way.

After acceptance, I took on forgiveness. A huge principle of AA is forgiving everything and everyone. Resentments are our number-one offender. If you hold on to your anger, it will take you out. It will eventually lead you back to drinking and using. At the cabin, they asked me to figure out *my* part in the resentment. Where had I been selfish, self-seeking, dishonest, or afraid?

You guys, I have a lot that I could look back and be angry about, such as what the "abortion money" guy did to me, or what Damon did to me, or what the producer at the W Hotel did to me. There was a lot that didn't feel like my fault at all. But the only thing in life that I had control over is myself and my reactions. I can't change my past. I'm allowed to be mad about these things, but I can also work to let them go. I can release the resentment and forgive. Because, honestly, my life depended on it—and I no longer wanted to die. I had purpose on this earth.

It was freeing.

I started to look at other people around me not as inherently bad or good, but rather as healthy or sick and doing the best they can. Everyone is doing their best. Sure, sometimes their best *sucks*, but that's okay.

I learned from AA that selfishness and self-seeking are the roots of all of my problems. I started to shift my thinking from what I could get to what I could give. When I felt depressed or suicidal or wanted to drink, they told me to ask myself who I've helped that day. Have I called my mom and asked how she was doing? Have I told a friend how much I appreciated them? I got really obsessed with buying homeless people sandwiches. Specifically, sandwiches. Thanks to the program, I had a new person to eat lunch with almost every day. This was my anti-depressant!

Then I started to feel . . . weird. I was smiling a lot? My jokes were less self-deprecating and more . . . joyful? What the fuck was happening to me?

Oh shit. This was happiness. I was *happy*. The fuck? Being sober was fun. Being single was fun. I didn't know that I could enjoy doing anything besides getting wasted. Holy fucking shit.

When I opened myself up to sobriety, things started to fall into place for me in my career. Soon after this, I booked a pilot on NBC called *A Mann's World*, written and directed by Michael Patrick King who wrote on *Sex and the City*. It was an amazing script. My character was supposed to be this vacant dumb model, but I took it a step further and gave her a really high, breathy, monotone voice and dead-eyed expression. Man, I really wasn't born to model, but I was beginning to think I was born to make fun of them. Then, the pilot didn't get picked up. But this time, I wasn't devastated. I was fine. This didn't feel like the end. I had met a bunch of amazing writers and actors through it. And I kept thinking about that character . . . who is she? What is she like when she goes to the grocery store? Sure, I didn't get to be on a pilot, but this was the inspiration for my Ivy character, who I still do all the time in my videos.

This pilot led to Michael Patrick King hiring me to guest star on *2 Broke Girls*. It was an incredible time in my life, when I felt like I was leading with faith instead of fear. I felt like the world was open to me. Every moment felt like an opportunity.

There was one day that I got locked out of my apartment. It was eleven a.m., and Jack was going to be at work until five. Normally I would have just cursed the world for twenty minutes, then found some drugs and got high to pass the time. But I was sober now. So . . . uh, shit. What do sober people do? What was second best to drugs? Ah yes. Coffee.

I walked down to the coffee shop on the corner of the street, ready to kill six hours until Jack got home to let me in. I got a coffee and sat down. I didn't have anything to read or work on or look at. GOD I WAS SO BORED. This would not do. I'm going to talk to people. I sat down at a table across from an eighty-year-old man that was also staring off into the distance. I asked him if I could sit . . . and then went on to tell him my life story. Then he told me his: he was an army veteran turned hot-air-balloon driver turned farmer. When he had to leave, I bought another coffee and sat down across from a woman I found out was a dancer turned dance instructor turned detective turned stay-at-home mom. I'm sure by my fourth hour of this, the introverts in the café were starting to be a bit afraid of me.

Then I saw a guy who looked weirdly familiar to me. I was FEELING THE COFFEE BUZZ to say the least, and I sat right down at his table.

"HI. YOU LOOK FAMILIAR," I said. "Do we know each other??"

"Uhhh. No." From his face you would have thought a wild monkey jumped down from the ceiling onto his table.

"Well anyway, I'm Laura and I got locked out of my apartment until like five p.m. tonight so I'm just here killing time—" I stopped, seeing his bewilderment. "Oh, sorry. Are you meeting someone?"

"Yeah, I am," he said, kind of annoyed.

"Oh. Sorry. Well I just thought you looked familiar! Bye!" I awkwardly backed away from his table. At least it was almost five p.m.! I walked back to my apartment to be let in.

A few weeks later I got a call from an unfamiliar number.

"Hey Laura, it's Peter!"

"Sorry . . . who?"

"Peter! We met at Kings Road Café a while ago. You just sat down at my table and started talking?"

"How did you get my number??"

"Well I figured out why I looked familiar to you. I'm friends with your sister's fiancé. We met at one of their parties."

"Oh! Okay cool." Where was this going?

Peter continued. "Anyway, I'm a director and I'm casting this series for AMC. I'd love for you to come in tomorrow and read for a role."

"Wow, I'd love to! What's the role?"

"Her name is Cornelia and she's a certifiably insane actress. I think you'd be perfect for it."

"I absolutely would be."

The next day, I went downtown and read for the role of Cornelia, the crazy actress, and booked it. Suddenly I was acting in a scene across from Jeffrey Tambor and Adam Goldberg in AMC's first digital series. We did three episodes and they never moved forward with the series, but it was okay. I had the tools to accept the things I couldn't change and appreciate the positive things that had come from this. Like, damn, I should get locked out of my apartment more often.

I'd be lying if I said that sobriety was a walk in the park. It was hard. Some days felt like they lasted forever. It made me isolate myself from my friends, who still loved to go out most nights. If I went out, I was afraid that I would drink. I was getting more and more lonely.

One night, I was tired of it. I was going to go on a date. I met this French guy at my yoga class a couple days before and he asked me out. It didn't hurt that he was very, *very* hot. I was compromising my form just to be able to sneak a peek at his downward dog, you guys. I'm not proud.

I called him to confirm our date. I was a little nervous about going out again, but I was sure I'd be fine. I had two months of sobriety by now! I pretty much had it in the bag. That's how that works, right?

He took me to a really fancy restaurant, where the portions are the size of your thumb and waiters put your napkins on your lap for you. Weird touch, but okay. After we sat down and were "napkined" by the waiter, my date took one glance at the menu and immediately asked, "May I have two glasses of your finest pinot noir?"

Oh shit. I can't drink wine. But also, damn what a sexy French accent. Focus, Laura. I opened my mouth to say something, but I was embarrassed. If I told him I was sober . . . what would he think? He'd see me as someone who can't control myself. Who can't handle alcohol like an adult. He'd see me as a child.

The waiter brought the wine over. I took it in my hand. He sipped his. I chugged mine.

Suddenly I was drunk and ordering more and more wine. I called the waiter over and slurred: "One more glass of peenwah, please? Just one more peenor. Thanks." I had relapsed.

By this point, the French guy was looking at me like I was crazy. But drunk-me took this look as bedroom eyes. "We should probably go back to your house, shouldn't we?" I asked.

"But this is the first date. Why are you so forward?"

I grabbed his shirt and yanked him toward me. "Because I am." Solid reasoning, drunk-me.

In addition to having a relapse, that date was a one-night stand.

The next day, I felt so . . . gross. It's like waking up from a nightmare, only to realize that everything you thought you dreamed actually happened. I was so ashamed. The entire two months of sobriety were gone, right before my eyes. I needed to do better.

It was in this moment that I started to understand that my addiction was a fatally progressive disease. It's not something that gets better with time. It's not something that I can beat. This would be something that I would have to tackle every single morning when I opened my eyes, and every night when I went to sleep.

Well, there goes my dating life! There was no way I was going out for a while. I just . . . I couldn't risk it. But whatever. I didn't need a guy anyway! Dating was fun, but ultimately I was enjoying being single. I went back into my antisocial cave, trying to gain back my confidence and consecutive days sober.

I slowly worked my way back up one day at a time. It was like training for the Olympics. I was exhausted, but I was doing it. The longer I went, the stronger I got. I dove into my work, and I barely even noticed the fact that I was . . . literally talking to no one. My friends had stopped trying to get me to come out with them. I was on their "do not call" list.

The only person who still bothered to try was my sister Colleen. She really made it her mission to incorporate me back into her life. All my other friends were afraid to push me out into the world, but Colleen knew that if I was going to ever lead a normal life as a sober person, I couldn't stay isolated all the time.

"Just go on a fucking date! Go!" she'd push me.

Fine. There was this entertainment lawyer named Ben who asked me out a few weeks ago. I could call him up and set up a date. So I did—I started seeing him. It was nice. He was busy with work and so was I. It was the perfect dating scenario for two people who put work before anything else. Canceling at the last minute was no problem. Awesome! Canceling at the last minute is my favorite thing to do. The only bad thing was that he didn't really understand my sobriety. He would say things like, "You can't just have ONE glass of wine with dinner? You can't just have ONE drink?"

Nope, I can't.

I didn't mind that he didn't completely understand me. I kind of thought no one ever would. Sobriety was something I did on my own. Ben and I saw each other pretty consistently—as consistently as two people in LA working in the industry can, but we weren't exclusive by any means.

I worked my way up to fifty-nine days sober again, seeing the lawyer on and off. And then Colleen called me. "Laura. Stop being such a bummer."

"I'm not a bummer! But I can't talk long, I'm going to bed soon."

"It's seven thirty."

"Your point?" There was a long pause. I could feel her judgment. "I need my ten hours!"

"Come out to my party tonight. Please. This isn't a request, it's a friendly demand. You're coming."

Colleen had found this group of friends in Los Angeles who were all British. She is a total anglophile. After two weeks of hanging out with them, she started speaking in a British accent, "Laura, would you like a spot of tea?" To which I would reply, "Colleen, you're from Chicago."

"Okay fine, I'll go. Let me see if Ben can come."

Ben was in. We planned to meet about an hour later to go to the party together. But five minutes before I was supposed to leave, Ben called me to say that he got busy with work and had to stay late tonight. This was . . . perfect! I called Colleen back. "Ben canceled, so I can't go tonight. Sorry!"

"Laura. You are your own fucking person and you can go out tonight by yourself."

"But—"

"YOU'RE AN ADULT."

Fine. I looked at Jack, who was currently passed out on the couch. He had one hand in a bag of Cheetos and the other down his pants, with a bong next to him. He was a messy gay stoner, but goddamn it, he was MY messy gay stoner. In a last-ditch effort, I pulled the pillow out from under his head to wake him up and took his bag of Cheetos away to use as leverage.

"Come with me to a party or the Cheetos go in the trash."

"Bitch, I'm sleeping!" He snatched the bag back, put a Cheeto in his mouth, and dozed off.

I guessed I was going alone. I made a mental plan to stay for an hour and then go straight home before I ruined everything.

I arrived at the party. It had a theme: "Dress the Way Your Parents Did When You Were Born." You might think this theme is oddly specific, but the last party was themed: "Wear an Outfit to Symbolize the Last Text You Sent"; and the one before that was "The Battle of 1812." I wanted to wear a hospital gown with my ass just completely out, because that's what my mom was wearing when I popped out . . . but I felt like the person with her ass out at the party can't also be the first person to leave. I was born in '86, so I found a pink-and-black-striped minidress, teased my hair, and slid on a bunch of bracelets. I called this look: "Phoned-In Eighties."

I parked my car outside her house and felt . . . stupid. I hate costume parties. Why would someone create an event where it's mandatory that you look dumb? I was wearing a stupid dress and I was going to go to this stupid party and drink stupid water because that's all I'm allowed to do.

I walked into the garden area and I remember seeing this man standing with a group of friends. He was wearing this really beautiful vintage suit and laughing at something someone said. Like really, truly laughing. I remember thinking he had a great smile. I wanted to know what he was laughing about. I bet I could make him laugh. Then I saw he was holding a bottle of water. Hmmm, I do need water. And I wanted to talk to him. I decided I'd ask him where he got that water. Smooth, right?

I used to go up to guys all the time in clubs. It's easy to talk to people! But, I had always been drunk before in these situations. This time I had no false confidence, no liquid courage. What was I going to say? Okay, Laura, just say words.

I had been standing in front of him and his group of friends, uncomfortably, for ten seconds already.

Awkwardly, I interrupted his conversation. "Where did you get your water?" He cocked his head to the side, smiling. He looked confused by the question, so naturally I continued: "BECAUSE I just love water. It's really important to stay hydrated, so I was just wondering where the water might be because water is my favorite beverage and I love it."

He raised an eyebrow and said, "Obviously you don't love water or else you would have brought some yourself."

"Are you accusing me of not loving water? I just wanted to sample the specific water at *this house*. I probably like water more than you."

"I'm just saying, if you loved it as much as you say you did, you would have brought it like I've brought mine," he said, grinning triumphantly. How did he get the upper hand here?

"All right. Whatever. I'm going to go find some water." I turned around and walked into the house. Real smooth, Laura. Man, I needed a drink. Of water.

I found my dumb water and sat down to socialize with all the party people. It was fun at first. But . . . then an hour or two passed and everyone had gotten progressively more drunk and high . . . this was my limit. I was a little annoyed, I'll admit. It was hard being the only sober person at a party. I didn't want to be a buzzkill, so I needed to get out of there.

I said my good-byes, and then figured I would find the water guy to say good-bye and catch him up on the fact that I found water immediately.

"I'm leaving!" I said to him, one arm reached out for an awkward side hug.

His smile dropped. "Oh, why are you leaving?"

"Because I'm the only sober person here!" I didn't mean to sound so annoyed. I looked at him apologetically. But he just looked excited—exuberant, in fact.

"I'm sober."

I was stunned. "*Sober* sober?" Because there's "I'm driving tonight" sober and there's also "if I have one drink I'll lose control and die" sober.

He smiled wide and nodded. "*Sober* sober."

"Stop it." I hadn't told him anything about myself, but suddenly we exchanged a look and it was like we knew more about each other than . . . anyone else. We had both been through the same war.

It was too long of a look. He cleared his throat. "Do you know of any good AA meetings around here? I just moved here and I don't know a lot of people or where to . . . stay focused."

"There's one at The Log Cabin. It's where I got sober. You should meet me there."

"Yeah. I will."

Damn. How awesome! Although that conversation would have been a lot weirder had I gone to the party ass-out. As I drove home,

175

I quietly thanked myself for not choosing that particular night to dress like an idiot.

The next day, Stephen met me outside The Log Cabin for the 11:30 a.m. meeting. We sat together inside, and afterward he asked me to lunch. At this time, I had been vegan for about year. But I always hated telling people this fact when I first met them. Because, you know, people hate vegans.

I was always pretty into vegetables and clean eating though, even during my addiction. At one point during my addiction I thought the more kale I consumed, the less cocaine I would crave. I realized that didn't work when I literally called my dealer from Veggie Grill.

But back to Stephen, what if he wanted to get barbecue or something? As we walked to a restaurant of his choice, I slid my veganism into the conversation.

"I don't really eat meat," I said.

"Oh, me neither," he replied.

Okay, maybe he didn't understand how serious I was about this. "I've been vegan for one year."

"I've been vegan for two years," he replied. *Are you kidding me?*

There were so many moments like this as we sat down and ate together. So many similarities between us. With Stephen I laughed more than I had in a long time. Suddenly three hours had passed. Oh shit, we were talking for three hours? I found out that he was a film composer, I heard about the town he was from, and I learned that his mom was a waitress and his dad worked in a furniture store.

That night, I called Colleen. "You'll never guess who I had lunch with today!"

"Who?"

"Stephen Hilton."

"Um. You can't date him."

I wasn't even thinking about dating him. It wasn't a date. I was just excited to have made a new friend. I mean, I really wasn't looking for a relationship. I was enjoying dating and being single. I was enjoying seeing (and canceling on) Ben. Hanging with Stephen was just . . . really, really fun lunches. As friends.

"It wasn't a date." I paused. "But also . . . why can't I date him?"

"He's married, Laura."

"Um . . . What?"

Now, I stand by the fact that I wasn't trying to date him. But . . . how had we talked for three hours with no mention of his wife? That was weird, right?

A week passed, and then Stephen asked if I wanted to go to the meeting together again. I said yes, but was still feeling weird about what my sister had told me. I sat weirdly far away from him during the meeting, and then he asked me to lunch again. I decided to give him a chance to tell me about his wife. I planned to really subtly slide it into conversation.

"So, have you ever been married?" I blurted out.

Stephen laughed. "Who told you that?"

"Colleen."

"I'm going through a divorce right now." He explained the whole situation to me. He married a woman in his early twenties and they had been separated for three years now. She lived across the world, back in London. He was completely honest. Come on, Colleen! You got me all worried over nothing.

Stephen asked me on a real date after that, and I really liked him. But . . . I was so excited to be single and not serious about anyone. I was living with my best friend in the world, going on auditions, and I felt strong. Why did I need a guy? The answer was . . . I didn't! So I avoided Stephen for a bit. He kept calling to ask me out, and I would put him off, I was working so much and getting so close to my goals that I could taste it.

I also knew that I really liked Stephen. If I went on a date with him . . . I was pretty sure I would want to keep dating him. Was I even ready for that? I kept putting him off, but Stephen was so kind and persistent. He called and asked if he could take me to dinner. I checked my calendar. . . . I was free, so I agreed to go.

And then . . . my agent called. "Laura, the producers scheduled a last-minute table read tomorrow for a pilot."

"Tomorrow?"

"Yep. Eight a.m. I'm having a production assistant bring by a new script for you. You should be getting it . . . about now."

KNOCK KNOCK. I opened the front door to see a nineteen-year-old boy with a large manila envelope in hand. Damn, my agent was good. "It's here," I said.

"Great. Study it, and I'll see you tomorrow. You're going to do great!"

Shit. I looked at the script. It was forty pages. I needed to study this so that I would do well tomorrow. Don't forget, I know what happens when you don't do well at the table read. They fire your ass and hire a fucking extra. Being that extra was awesome, but I'd rather not experience the other side of it. I called Stephen to cancel. I felt bad—I had already canceled on him twice. But this was important; this was my career.

"Hey Stephen, have you left yet?"

"Yeah, I'm on my way!"

Damn it. Okay, I wasn't going to cancel on him if he was already on the way to pick me up. Traffic in LA is no joke. I thought quickly.

"Okay well, I can only stay out for one hour. I have to study for this table read I have in the morning. I hope you understand."

"No problem, Laura! See you soon!"

Damn his good-natured flexibility. A few years later he confessed to me that he hadn't actually left yet. He was standing in his kitchen during the call. He just knew I was going to cancel again so he lied. Sneaky, but also effective.

He took me to a sushi restaurant where they have a really good vegan roll. They sat us next to the bar, so the two vegans on a date got to watch fish get butchered while we ate. Then I spilled sauce all over the waitress. I was nervous! Not only was this a date, but I was so anxious about the table read. I think it was getting to me. I got kind of quiet.

"Are you all right?" Stephen asked me.

"I don't feel great. Will you tell me some funny stories?"

So he did. He rattled off one about the single day he worked in a furniture store before getting fired, and one about a local convenience store he used to frequent in London where when he'd check out, the guy behind the counter would always, no matter what, ask if he wanted "anything else?" For some reason, Stephen and his friends were determined to get this guy to stop saying "anything else?" After every purchase. So the next time Stephen bought a banana, he said sternly, "I'll get this banana and ABSOLUTELY NOTH-ING else." There was a long stare-off between Stephen and the guy behind the counter. Then . . . "Anything else?" the guy behind the counter replied. He told me story after story, each more hilarious than the next. I was laughing my ass off, then I had a scary thought:

Is he funnier than me? Oh shit, I'm supposed to be the funny one in my relationships. I was so worried about it that later on I called my mom, all butthurt. "Mom . . . I think he's funnier than me."

To which she replied, "Oh no, Laura, is he sweet and sensitive, too? How terrible for you."

"I'm the funny one, Mom! *I'm the funny one!*"

She didn't have any sympathy for me regarding this amazing guy I had met. Early on, I would even try to suppress my laughter when he told a funny joke. Like seriously, comedy is my job! He's the music person—it's not like I ever got on the piano in front of him and told him I was a musical genius. Why did he have to be so good at everything?

Fortunately, my silly jealousy was hard to keep up when I was laughing this hard. Also, his humor is one of the things I love most about him. Besides, I maintain that I am the funnier one in the relationship.

We finished dinner and went outside, waiting for the valet to bring Stephen's car around. I noticed he was shaking. He was so nervous. He looked at me and asked, "Can I kiss you?" Oh my God. No one had ever asked me that before. *What the fuck do I say? I should be coy. No, I should be . . . flirtatious.* I squinted my eyes halfway closed, which was my best attempt at a sensual expression. "What do you think?" I growled. Pretty dope, right?

He leaned forward a bit, then stopped. Oh God, I had confused him. "Um. Does that—uh . . ." Stephen stuttered. Finally, he leaned in for a nice, soft kiss.

From that moment on, I didn't see Ben again.

Falling in love with Stephen was sweet and perfect. Since we were both sober, we decided to go café hopping instead of bar hopping. We walked along Ocean Avenue in the afternoon and went from one café to the next, getting coffees and juices and different pastries at each one. I told him about my parents; my sisters; and about the fact that ever since I was little, I've woken up at three a.m. every night to eat a green apple. I still do that for some reason.

At the end of one of these dates, he asked if I wanted to come back to his apartment to watch a movie.

I narrowed my eyes at him. "Yes, but do not try anything funny with me!" I was a changed woman, you guys. With him, I didn't want to mess anything up. We had gone on several dates by now, and I wanted to take things slow. Super slow, like the tortoise who won that race or whatever? I just mean I wasn't fucking him yet.

We got back to his apartment and he put on *Dr. Strangelove*. I think he was trying to impress me. No shade to Stanley Kubrick, but I was more in the mood for something like *Happy Gilmore*. I'm sorry! Sometimes I have to turn off my brain. This was just really dry and really boring. I looked at him. "This is terrible."

"It's really bad, isn't it?" he replied.

We put on another movie called *Bad Timing*. It still wasn't Adam Sandler, but it was good enough. When it ended, it was really late.

"You look tired," he said to me. "Just spend the night. I don't want you driving all the way home this late."

I thought about it. I felt so comfortable with him at this point, and I really was tired. "Okay, I could do that."

I went to sleep easily in his bed. At three a.m., I heard something in the kitchen. I got a little scared and drowsily scanned the room . . . I opened my eyes a bit and noticed Stephen wasn't in bed anymore. Then I saw his figure walk into the bedroom, out of breath . . . and he set down a green apple on my bedside table. I smiled and fell back asleep.

In the morning I found out that he had driven to three different convenience stores at three in the morning, looking for an apple for me. (And absolutely nothing else.) "They were all closed, but finally I found one that was still open and carried apples. Tough combination, it turns out!"

It was the sweetest thing. The apple, I mean. They were in season at that time.

But yeah, obviously we had sex after that. I'm not a monster.

I was totally and completely in love. I started to feel more carefree than I ever had been since I got sober. It was like he was teaching me how to have fun and let loose. Before, letting loose meant risking my life.

Time went on and I finally achieved six months completely sober. I felt like I could do this thing called life. I could do anything! I felt so loved and in love. Every week I would go to my meeting at The Log Cabin. Every morning I would get on my knees and ask God-as-I-know-it to keep me sober for the day. Every day I would talk to other sober people to stay grounded. I was working through the 12 Steps. I was on Step 8. We made a list of all persons we had harmed, and became willing to make amends to them all. 'Twas a very long list. . . . But yeah, eight out of twelve seemed pretty good. I felt like I was almost done.

But "being done" doesn't ever happen with addiction. If I wasn't actively focused on recovery, my addiction would creep up and become my solution to life's problems. They say in AA that anything you put before sobriety, you'll lose. I heard them . . . but I didn't feel like losing anything was possible now. Slowly, I started putting Stephen first. I didn't really notice it. As time went on, I started thinking to myself, *If I can go six months without picking up drugs or having a drink, then I can afford to miss my weekly meeting. I can stop getting on my knees in the morning and asking my higher power to keep me sober. I can stop talking to other sober people.*

I stopped for eight days, but those tools were what quieted down the voice of my addiction. By the eighth day of not applying those tools, the voice of my addiction started to get very loud. It wasn't even a particularly bad day. Stephen and I didn't have a fight; I didn't get a rejection; I didn't lose a job.

I was at my apartment trying to write, but I had writer's block. Jack was at work. *Damn it, what do I write, what do I write?* Then I figured out the solution. *Oh, I know what will help.* Some of Jack's weed. It was like an out-of-body experience. I went into Jack's dresser drawer, pulled out his stash of weed, and smoked it. I coughed heavily. It had been a while.

Well, fuck. Now I had smoked weed and ruined six fucking months of sobriety. I might as well go buy some beer. I got some beer and drank it. Well, I'm already drunk. I might as well buy some cocaine.

I had deleted the numbers of every drug dealer I knew, but no one is unreachable in the age of Facebook! I found one of my old connects, hit him up via Facebook messenger, and picked some up.

I snorted some cocaine. I might as well smoke it, too.

Now I was finally cracked out of my mind—jittery and shaking like the crackheads you see on the street. I didn't even feel good. The shame still seeped through the numbness. How the fuck was it doing that? The weight of my situation came crashing down on me. I lay in my bed, staring at the ceiling and feeling meaningless. I ruined my sobriety. I ruined my life. I might as well die.

I went to the drug store and bought some sleeping pills. I took seven pills. I didn't care if I lived or died. If I didn't wake up, then I didn't wake up. Who fucking cares? I knew that the mix of uppers and downers had the capacity to stop my heart. It's very dangerous to take them together. That's how Heath Ledger died. I knew this and I didn't care about the risk. But still, if I really wanted to die, wouldn't I have taken the whole bottle? Come on, Laura, commit for once!

After I took the pills, I went from cracked out to knocked out. I was supposed to see Stephen that night for a date. When I didn't show up, he kept calling and calling me, with no answer. Immediately he knew I had relapsed. It wasn't like me to not show up to a date without calling.

Jack got home from work, saw me passed out on my bed, and just assumed I had fallen asleep. The next day I woke up and my whole body hurt. I saw I had twenty missed calls from Stephen. I called him immediately.

He answered, but there was only silence on the line. Eventually he spoke. "You relapsed, didn't you?"

"Yeah." I wished more than anything that I could have said no. I wished that I had just fucking lost my phone, or gotten a concussion, or gone into a coma. Anything but this.

He sounded so disappointed. In the most gentle way possible, Stephen told me that he couldn't be with me if I wasn't sober. No matter how much he loved me and wanted to take care of me, his sobriety had to come first.

I had to fight the voice that told me it was useless to go back to my sobriety. The voice said it was hopeless to try again. That it was pointless to want to live. I went back to Alcoholics Anonymous to try again. They say that you aren't supposed to get sober for anyone else in your life besides yourself, but . . . I couldn't bear to lose

Stephen. So I went back to The Log Cabin, even though I felt like I wasn't worth shit.

As I entered, I saw this woman across the room. She had this huge presence. Even before I talked to her, I could tell she was a force of nature. She was this curvy girl in a tiny, tiny dress and she was glowing. I mean, her contour game was strong. I felt pulled toward her and sat down next to her. We started talking and I found out her name was Kristal. I don't know what it was about her, but I found myself telling her everything. "Yeah, I relapsed but I'm back now. It's fine. I'm only twenty-three. I'm young."

She said, unflinchingly, "If you don't take this seriously, you're going to die." She was facing me dead-on. She wasn't smiling. She didn't feel sorry for me. "You're not too young to die."

"I—" I held her gaze. "Good morning to you too." She didn't laugh at my joke.

"Last week I buried a girl just like you. A funny, pretty blonde. She was twenty-three too. OD'd in her bathtub. You're not invincible. This will take you down just like it took her."

When she said that, it hit me. Something about Kristal and the way she spoke to me got through. I believed everything she said.

"I'm afraid of you. Will you sponsor me?" I knew she wouldn't let me get away with anything. She nodded yes, and I was completely recommitted.

I spoke to her in person or on the phone every single day. I started the steps over again. I gave it everything I had. I did it like my life depended on it, because now I truly knew that it did.

Kristal helped me take inventory of everything in my life: every defect, every fear, every resentment. I wrote it all down in this thick yellow journal, that—by the end of the inventory—was as battered as I felt. Kristal made sure I was thorough: tackling, investigating, and dealing with everything inside myself. Kristal just gave and gave to me, without compensation or condition.

Something shifted in my mind and changed how I perceived the world. I felt like I finally woke up, like I could see the world more clearly now as a place of love instead of a place of survival or of fear. I focused on living through serving others, rather than for myself. My new mantra was trust God, clean house, help others.

Trust God meant that I needed to trust the power of the universe/penguins and stop trying to run the fucking show. Ultimately, I don't have control over everything in the world, or really much at all. Accepting that brings peace.

Clean house meant that I needed to check in every day with myself to ask: Am I resentful? Do I owe amends? Have I been selfish, self-seeking, dishonest, or afraid? If so, what's a better way? It meant making sure that my side of the street is clean. It's also about recognizing the good in my life. Seeing what I can be grateful for around me.

Help others . . . that's pretty self-explanatory, isn't it? It's so simple, but it's a huge part of my sobriety. I started giving to others what was so freely given to me. Kristal, this force of nature in a tiny dress, gave hours and hours of her time to me to teach me how to live without drinking. So I did the same for others. In all parts of my life, I tried to focus outward rather than inward.

This was a huge shift for me. I had been so self-obsessed. Completely consumed with what I could get rather than what I could give. Everything was about MY NEEDS. I needed scar cream. I needed to be successful. I needed the lead role in the pilot. This self-absorption led me to be completely riddled with fear—I might not get what I needed, and I could even lose what I had. It made me miserable. When I made my day about being rigorously honest and giving, I felt happy.

I feel blessed that I had the willingness to change. It doesn't happen unless you're willing, and there are so many people around me that succumbed to their illnesses. I don't know why I'm still alive. I mean, you read the previous chapters—you know what I was up to. But thanks to Kristal and a swift kick in the ass, I have a design for living now that works for me. If I don't do it every day, I get sicker.

One of the many slogans in AA is: "You can't get clean off yesterday's shower." One day with no shower: tolerable. Two days: yuck. Three days: you're just plain offensive.

Trust God, clean house, help others. Every day.

As I got more and more days sober under my belt, Stephen and I started seeing each other again. He was cautious, and I completely understood. He didn't know if I was going to stick with the program. I had proven myself to be unreliable. All I could do was keep going and keep proving to him that I could live a sober life.

—

On my thirtieth day of sobriety, I got a call from Peter, the director I harassed at that coffee shop. "Laura, I'm doing a movie in New York with Jason Bateman and Olivia Wilde and I want you to be in it. I don't have complete say in casting, so you just need to make a self-tape audition, and make it good. I can get you the job."

I sent in the self-tape . . . and booked it! But there were some conditions.

"We would love to have you on set. The only thing is that it's an indie."

"That's . . . fine? Right?"

"Well. It means that we can't afford to fly you out here or put you up. If you can make it to New York and find a place to stay for a month, then you have the job."

Okay, well, I had no money to do that. I had blown it all on drugs. So I figured that was that. I couldn't do it. I told Stephen, and he couldn't believe I was passing up an opportunity like this.

"But . . . you love Jason Bateman!"

"I know!"

"Can I give you some money to go?" he offered. I frowned—I really didn't want to make him give me money. "You have to do this, Laura. It's your career." I hugged him. I didn't know what I'd do without Stephen—and I was only going to take the bare minimum, no more. My oldest sister Tracy, who I haven't spoken enough about in this book, also lent me money to make sure I had enough to eat during the month of shooting. Tracy was always like a second mom to me growing up. As irritating as she found me, she was always there to help. No questions asked.

Okay, now I had the money to buy a plane ticket and pay for food while in New York. There was no way in hell I could afford a hotel for a month. I posted a Facebook status: "Who the hell do I know that lives in New York?" I got one response—from Claire, a girl I haven't talked to since we did speech together in high school.

"Yooooo, Claire! How have you been for the past eight years? By the way, I'm going to be in New York for a month. Do you think I could uh . . . stay with you?"

"No problem!"

Wow, this wasn't going to be weird at all!

Cut to . . . my first night sleeping over in her apartment. Claire's smiling face was one foot away from mine, as we lay together in her double bed in her tiny Manhattan studio apartment. It was the size of a closet. And it had no closet. I'm pretty sure it *was* a closet.

"How's your mom?" I asked. I figured that if I was lying this close to someone else's face, then I should probably talk to them.

"Good," she replied. "Remember how early we had to get up on Saturdays? That was fun."

"Totally."

"Yeah."

"Sure."

To make things a bit more difficult, the first thing Claire offered me when I got in her apartment was weed. I politely said no. *Okay, I cannot stay here for a whole month.*

As I was walking from Claire's apartment to the set the next day, I was overcome with fear. New York City had been the place where my addiction had reared its ugly head for the first time. It was where I fell into Damon's grasp. I had no fond memories here. How was I going to stay sober here alone? I didn't have The Log Cabin, I didn't have Kristal or Stephen or anyone. Plus it was a bit awkward to get on my knees in the morning and ask God to keep me sober for the day, with Claire five feet away making toast next to the toilet.

A week passed in Claire's closet apartment, and I remembered that Michael, a friend whose short film I acted in, had moved to New York the year before. I stepped into the hallway and hit him up immediately to ask if he had any extra space I could stay in.

"Totally, dude! You can stay on the couch in our basement."

Thank God. I thanked Claire profusely for letting me stay with her, and then went to the other house in Brooklyn. I was nervous: this was going to be a whole group of new people I'd have to meet and socialize with and live with for the next three weeks. If I was going to be uncomfortable, how would I be certain I wouldn't drink?

I walked into the house and set my stuff down. Then Michael's roommate, Leslie, walked in and introduced herself. We talked for a moment, and then she said:

"Welp. Off to AA bishes."

"Wait, what!!"

"Yeah, I've been sober six months."

"I've been sober almost two months!"

She smiled at me; she understood. "Come with me!"

From then on, I went with her every day that I was in New York. It was inexplicable, like there was something watching over me. In AA, we call that a God shot.

New York was a success. I played a dumb model named Bunny. What the fuck was up with the model thing? I did my Ivy character for it again.

I came back to LA on a high, feeling stronger than ever. Stephen felt it, too. We got back together. Things were good again.

"Move in with me?" he asked one day while we were laying on his couch, watching *Millionaire Matchmaker*. We had been dating for around five months.

I smiled and kissed him. "Aw, I'd love to. But no."

I didn't want to move in with another guy until I was married. Not because I was traditional or anything, I just really hate moving. I didn't want to change locations unless I knew I would be living with this person for the rest of my life. It wasn't a marriage ultimatum. Moving is just a real pain in the ass.

"Fair enough," he replied.

A month later, he took me out to this beautiful restaurant called Inn of the Seventh Ray.

"Why?" I asked.

"Why what?"

"Why are you taking me to such a nice place on a Wednesday night?"

"Because I love you and I just want to take you somewhere, okay?"

"Okay, okay, sorry!"

The waiter seated us at a table, handed us menus, and then stepped away. Oh wait, I wanted sparkling water. I turned around to look for the waiter, couldn't find him, and turned back to Stephen, who was gone from his seat. Wait, where did he go?

"Oh shit."

Stephen was down on one knee in front of me. He was shaking with nerves as he opened the ring box. "Will you marry me? I love you." He stood up.

"Wait—you can't stand up yet! You've gotta wait until I answer."

"Right, right. Sorry." He knelt back down.

"YES!"

We got married one year after we met. The thought of either of us planning a wedding felt like the biggest joke in the world, so we just eloped and flew to Anacapri in Italy the next day. That was it. It felt easy, simple, and right.

CHAPTER 9

Two Apartments and a Home

I moved into Stephen's small one-bedroom apartment in Santa Monica shortly after he proposed to me. We were so in love. Since both of us had jobs with irregular hours, we could stay in bed a bit longer in the morning, watching the sunlight streak into the room.

BANG! BANG! BANG!

This morning, our peace was broken by an angry-looking old woman hitting our window with a broom. I quickly pulled the sheet over my body. What the hell? She peered in through our window.

"Stephen! RENT IS DUE IN TWO DAYS. DO NOT FORGET!" she yelled with a thick Russian accent. She spotted me and glared. Or maybe that was her resting face? It was unclear.

When Stephen moved to America he had no credit. So no sane landlord would let him rent from them. Which is why he ended up with:

"DO NOT FORGET, Stephen! TWO! DAYS!" She punctuated the last two words with whaps of the broom against the window.

Stephen and I shrank down under the covers, waiting for her to leave. This overbearing Russian woman and her weird codependent daughter let Stephen rent from them because he is British. "These Americans are up to no good. You come with us," they'd said. Stephen wasn't really in a place to say no. I guess the landlord wasn't accustomed to texting or phone calls or ringing the doorbell. Her communications were always through our window: "Stephen! Sweep the front porch. IT IS VERY DIRTY."

They had bought this apartment complex in the '70s for dirt cheap. These tiny apartments were built in the 1920s, absolutely about to fall apart, but cute nonetheless. The old woman lived in the front one, we lived in the second one, another family lived in the third one, and the daughter lived alone in the last one.

The mother and daughter would fight constantly. They were both codependent and hated each other. The old lady was always convinced there was going to be a war. One time, when we were invited into the old woman's apartment, I used the bathroom and saw that her bathtub was completely filled with fruit. They hoarded so much food. When there was a news report about a bombing in London, the old lady ran to Stephen's window and offered to let his entire family stay with them here. "We can keep them safe for when the war comes. We have bathtub of fruit. They will be okay."

"What war? This was just a random attack."

Her face darkened: "There will be war, Stephen."

As overbearing as she was, there was only one moment where she truly crossed the line. She popped up in the window holding a plastic bag. "Stephen, you must try these apples I just bought."

Stephen awkwardly reached through the open window and grabbed one. "All right, thanks." She then went on to insist he take a bite while also saying, "I do not like Laura. She is not right for you. You must leave her. She is not the one!"

Luckily, I wasn't there at the time, but Stephen recounted the story to me later. "I don't know what came over me, but I was so upset and offended that I pointed at her and said, 'DO NOT EVER SPEAK LIKE THAT ABOUT THE WOMAN I LOVE.' And then she nodded respectfully. I think she gets it now."

"Wow. We're like Romeo and Juliet, but if your family was the landlord and there wasn't really anything at stake."

"Yes, that's exactly it." Stephen nodded. We had a good laugh. Stephen's such a gentle creature, it takes a lot to get him to yell.

There were so many similarities between Stephen and me. We always joked that we were from different countries but the same town. Stephen grew up in Faversham, this suburb outside of London; I was from a suburb outside of Chicago. The towns even look strangely similar, with their long front yards and brick buildings. We both grew up working-class, his dad was employed at a furniture store and his mother was a waitress.

Stephen is half Irish and half British. In the 1960s his father moved to London from a very poor town in Southern Ireland. His name was Sean Murphy, and it really doesn't get more Irish than that. When Sean was looking for work, every business had a sign up that said: No dogs, no Blacks, no Irish.

When he was walking home from another unsuccessful day looking for work, he looked up and saw the Hilton Hotel. Hilton, he decided, sounds British. He proceeded to change his name from Sean Murphy to John Hilton. He got rid of his accent and finally found a job ushering in a movie theater. He met his wife-to-be Mavis when they were both working as ushers. They got married and had

Stephen. Then the three of them moved into this tiny one-bedroom apartment together until they moved into the slightly bigger two-bedroom town house, which they still have today.

There's something about growing up the same way that gives you a deep connection. We both unconsciously poured water into the dish soap to make it last longer and had parents who didn't pressure us to go to college. Instead they supported our artistic endeavors even though the odds were against us.

Stephen will sometimes look at me with fear in his eyes and ask, "What if we go bankrupt and lose our house and our careers?"

I'll just smile at him and say, "Then we'll move to a cheap city and get a one-bedroom apartment and have a baby and I'll still make comedy and you'll still make music and we'll still be in love and happy."

Stephen will smile back at me, then. "That sounds bloody rubbish, doesn't it?"

It does a bit.

Stephen's mom raised him on pop music. She'd have the radio blasting, and Stephen would contribute by banging pots and pans. When he got older, he traded the cooking utensils for piano, and then piano for synthesizers. By the time he was a teenager, he was creating elaborate musical soundscapes in his room alone, not coming out until he was satisfied with what he'd made.

When high school rolled around, his mother would drop him at the entrance of the school and he would immediately walk out the back door. He was completely over it—there was just no way he was going. He had music dreams to make happen, and they did not feature algebra.

He completed his angsty demeanor with all-black outfits and dark eyeliner. He and his friends would drop acid, travel to London, and walk around at four in the morning. One early morning when they were taking an acid-walk, a cop stopped them. "What's going on?" the cop asked after blocking their path.

Pupils dilated, Stephen smiled at him. "We have emotional problems."

The cop stepped forward menacingly. "It's four in the morning, bud. You got drugs in your pockets?"

He and his friends looked at each other . . . then ran! Hey, Stephen didn't have time to get arrested—he had a music career to attend to. When he was fifteen years old, he got a record deal, dropped out of high school, and moved to London. The record label put him up in this abandoned, repurposed church attic, where he would sit alone and compose music twenty-four hours a day. I'm not exaggerating. He started taking speed to keep himself awake and working, and he became addicted to it. In that music scene it's common, even celebrated, to go to work fucked up. I can't speak for him, but I'd guess that it's even harder to realize you have a problem and fix it when you're submerged in that world, surrounded by people who are also fucked up all the time.

Stephen really had his own crazy story. He'd start every morning with straight vodka, and pepper it through the day with drugs to keep the high sustained. He was even worse than me when he finally woke up from his addiction. But thank God, he did. He changed himself and figured out how to create music and use his genius without supplementing it all with drugs.

A short while before I met him, he got a call from Hans Zimmer.

Hans said that he loved Stephen's music and he wanted him to come out to LA to compose films with him. So Stephen hopped on a plane and came out here. It was that simple. I mean, when Hans Zimmer tells you to move, you move.

That's when I met him. He was eight years sober. When we got engaged, when we got married, I had never even seen what Stephen was like when he was drinking or using. If he had been using, he wouldn't have been able to handle the pressure of working under Hans Zimmer, he wouldn't have moved out to LA, I wouldn't have met him or liked him, and we wouldn't have been together in this one-bedroom apartment cuddled up on the couch, peacefully ready for the rest of our lives, with our crazy Russian landlady skulking outside the window.

When things got more financially stable for us, we moved out of our one-bedroom apartment and into a two-bedroom apartment in Santa Monica. It was beautiful, with big windows and sunlight and a kitchen that wasn't super-busted. But . . . our neighbors at the new place made us miss the Russian lady and her bathtub of fruit.

Our downstairs neighbors had this strange energy about them. They were full-on hoarders living in filth, and they were so angry all the time. Stephen and I held our breath while passing their front door. "Their scent makes me appreciate the sweet smell of our apartment even more!" Stephen would say, trying to look at the bright side. They paid only four hundred dollars a month because of rent control. Both of them just stayed in the apartment all day, every day. They barely ever came out.

Since they were on the bottom floor, they had free rein of the front yard, where they kept their huge, angry dogs. The dogs would lunge at anyone who passed in front of their apartment, and they would only be stopped by this tiny little gate that looked like it was weakening with every lunge. It was terrifying. Their rabid barking would be our morning alarm clock and our soothing bedtime soundtrack. *But tell me all about that bright side again, Stephen?*

Then, next door to us was this sweet young family with two children, ages one and three. The dogs would lunge at the kids every time they left their apartment. The family would constantly ask the hoarders to put their dogs inside, and the hoarders would ask them to go die. Stephen and I had moved into the middle of a full-on feud.

One day, the barking from downstairs stopped. Wait, how was I supposed to sleep without their vicious barking? I was used to it now, and the silence was unsettling. The next day, the young mom knocked on our door with tears in her eyes.

"So . . . I called animal services on the dogs."

"Ohhh, that's why things have been so peaceful here!"

She nodded sadly. "I wasn't trying to be mean! I had to. They just kept lunging at little Elliot. So . . . they got back at us by calling Child Protective Services on us and said we were abusing our children."

Damn, that was cold. "Oh no."

The woman continued shakily, "And the worst part is that little Elliot just fell and hit his head and . . . he has a . . . a . . . BLACK EYE." She started sobbing. "So if anyone from Child Protective Services comes to your door, can you tell them Jeff and I are—are good parents?"

"Yes, yes of course." She hugged me for an awkwardly long time.

It was a fucking weird place. Beautiful apartment, though! Big windows.

We had been married a year and a half when we were in this apartment, and both of our careers started to get really busy. Stephen was doing well at work, which meant he was getting more responsibility, which meant more pressure. He slowly started to change. At first, he just became reclusive, staying awake at his keyboard, figuring out musical cues until late into the night. I'd go to sleep alone in our bed and wake up much earlier than him to pray and meditate and go to yoga. We were on completely different schedules. I'd eat dinner at seven, and he . . . well, I wouldn't even see him eat. He would bring all food to his desk.

He became more testy when things would go wrong. Things used to roll off his back so easily before, but now he fixated on his mistakes and became angry and frustrated . . . and then mean and spiteful to me.

Then he spiraled further. He would bang his head against the wall as hard as he could after trying to come up with a particular tricky cue for a film. I wondered if he was losing his mind. *Who the fuck is this person?* In the back of my mind, I wondered whether he had relapsed and was hiding it. I never knew Stephen when he was using. I had been a different person when I was using, so maybe this was Stephen on drugs.

Things were tense between us. We would fight constantly, with me wondering what the hell was going on and him in complete denial of his state. One day we were having a particularly loud yelling match in our apartment and I heard a knock at the door.

It was the young mother from next door. "I heard you guys yelling."

I awkwardly wiped the tears from my eyes. "Um, I'm sorry. We can quiet down."

"No, no, I get it. I understand." She pulled a book out of her purse.

The title read, *Mating in Captivity: Unlocking Erotic Intelligence*. "I wanted to give this to you."

I read the back cover. "*Mating in Captivity* takes a hard line against one of the most time-honored institutions in human history . . . the sexless marriage?"

She looked at me sympathetically. "It helps."

I just stared at her, dumbfounded. "Thanks?" I shut the door.

I later found out that Stephen had stopped going to meetings. He stopped praying and meditating and calling his sponsor in the morning. He wasn't using the tools we had both built for ourselves. Those steps are like insulin for a diabetic; if we weren't actively doing them, we were getting sicker. In the absence of those tools, the voice of his addiction got really loud, and suddenly, just like I had during my relapse, he had forgotten the healthy tools he had used to solve life's problems. Suddenly, he didn't know how to deal with his stress. He became riddled with anxiety and fear that he couldn't cope with.

Soon enough, a psychiatrist was prescribing him anti-anxiety medication and sleeping pills. In the back of his mind, he knew that he didn't have the ability to take this kind of medication safely. He knew, but he also needed the pain and bad feelings to stop. There was another way to do this, but he couldn't remember it. He just needed to be able to work. He could tackle his deeper issues later on, right? He just needed to get this music cue out to Hans, *now*.

Before he knew it, he had relapsed. He was abusing the medication. One day, I was working in the kitchen and Stephen was in the bathroom. I heard the faint rattling of a pill bottle. Immediately, I understood what was going on.

He was going completely insane, and I didn't know what to do about it. He wouldn't listen to me anymore. He would take his bike out at three in the morning to "get some French fries at Swingers" and come back completely bloody and fucked up. There was one morning that I was leaving for an important shoot. We were shooting a pilot that I wrote. This was big for me! As I grabbed my keys, Stephen began to smash his head into the door, threatening to kill himself if I left. It was such a fucked-up time. I was scared. I pulled him into the car with me and dropped him off at the emergency room, not knowing whether he would be dead or alive when I got back. I knew I couldn't help him. Addiction is something that you can only pull yourself out of. It's the only way.

I called Kristal and told her what was happening. I knew that I couldn't be around him if he was using. With Stephen's sobriety gone, I immediately knew that my sobriety was at risk too. Though I never stopped loving him, I couldn't be with an active addict, and I didn't sign up to take this sort of abuse. It wouldn't be long before his addiction would transfer onto me. I started looking for an apartment to move into alone.

I didn't tell him anything because of how emotionally unstable he was. He was threatening to kill himself. After hearing that so often in my past from Damon, the threat felt very real to me. I didn't feel safe telling him I was leaving, but I found a small place in Venice and contacted them to rent it.

The day before I had planned to leave, Stephen came home, panicked and out of breath and fucked up. Completely fucked up. But behind his eyes there was a glimmer of him. He wasn't completely gone, I could tell.

He spoke rapidly. "I'm done. I'm done. I'm done. I can't do this anymore. I heard a voice and it told me to stop and I have to stop. I have to stop." He ran into the bathroom, took his bottle of Xanax and flushed all the pills down the toilet. Which by the way, you're not supposed to do. It's bad for the ocean. Sorry, fishies.

Maybe he subconsciously knew that I was leaving. I'm not sure. We got into bed that night, and he was shaking and twitching and sweating. He looked so sick, like he was on the verge of something really bad. He was staring at the ceiling completely terrified, flinching every so often. I didn't know what he was seeing. He took my hand. "There's dark clouds all around me. I'm scared, Laura."

I was so scared. I got out of bed and called a friend in the program. Frantically I told her that Stephen had thrown all his Xanax away and was seeing things and shaking. She said that he was going through withdrawal.

Stephen had been abusing Xanax, and this particular drug forces your body to depend on it. If you quit cold turkey, you can have a seizure and die. You have to medically detox from it, especially from the amount Stephen was taking. I looked over to him, the twitching was getting worse. His heart was racing. I took his hand and led him to my car and sped to the hospital.

I was terrified that Stephen could have a seizure at any minute. What if he had one in the car while I was driving? What would I do? I couldn't even think. We got to the emergency room and saw a doctor who didn't understand addiction at all. He looked at us like Stephen was the scum of the earth. "Why can't you control how much you take? What is wrong with you?"

I was enraged, and Stephen wasn't even coherent.

"He needs help. He's sick." My voice was shaking with anger.

"He had a prescription. Just FOLLOW it." This doctor was a piece of work.

"Please, just help us," I said, trying my hardest not to punch this guy's eyes out.

The doctor glared at us both and said, "I'll be back."

Where was he going, to take a fucking smoke break?!

Stephen couldn't speak, but I could tell he was scared for his life. He was barely coherent but I could see him in there, trying to fight his way through this. Suddenly his back arched, his fists clenched, his body seized up completely. He had gone into a full-on seizure, shaking and jerking so hard he almost fell off the table. He turned blue.

I screamed as loud as I could for someone to get in here NOW. Stephen went stiff. The doctors and nurses raced in the room and put the defibrillator on his chest.

I was screaming. I couldn't stop screaming. Two nurses grabbed my arms. "You need to leave, ma'am."

"No! No!" I yelled.

The doctor rubbed together the sides of the defibrillator. "CLEAR!" I watched Stephen's chest arch with the electric current as I was torn from the room.

They put me in an empty waiting room down the hall.

I begged and cried, but they wouldn't let me out. I couldn't stop picturing Stephen's stiff body and blue face. I thought he was dead. I paced and paced, every minute felt like an hour. I was terrified that I had lost him. After twenty minutes a nurse came in the room.

"We stabilized him, but he needs to medically detox immediately. You have to take him to a rehabilitation center right now."

"Okay. Okay."

"We've given him some anti-seizure medication, so he should be fine for a bit, but you need to go right away."

Wait, I had to drive him? In my car, which was not equipped with emergency medical equipment or personnel? How were we going to make it there?

I must have pulled out my phone and called some rehab centers, but at that point, I was on autopilot. My hands and feet were moving without me. I wasn't in my body. I found a rehab center in Tarzana that would take Stephen, and I got him in the car. He was so out of it, he didn't recognize me. I started the car, but I was so petrified he was going to have another seizure. I was so afraid he was going to die in the car, but I just drove. I had to get him there.

We made it there without incident, and he went straight into the medical detox program for thirty days.

I stayed in our two-bedroom apartment in Santa Monica for those thirty days. I talked to his mom every day about how he was doing. I went to visit him when visitors were allowed, but I still kept my plan to move into that Venice apartment. The thing is, I didn't know if he was going to stay sober after he got out of this program. A medical detox safely brings you back to sobriety, but it was up to Stephen to stay that way. I didn't know who he was going to be when he came out of this. He needed to get sober and get better, and I couldn't be responsible for that. No one could get him sober except him.

At the end of the thirty days, I went to pick him up. He looked like himself again. He told me that he didn't feel ready to be out in the world, so he had decided to go to an all-male rehab facility. I smiled, because that showed me he had a lot of willingness to get better. He knew that he had been inches away from death, and he saw everything he had to lose. He was timid and kind, and a lot closer to the Stephen I knew before, but the scars from the past months were still there. I hadn't forgotten how he treated me.

I dropped him off at the rehab facility and went back to our apartment. He started on the 12 Steps again. Fifteen days after he began rehab, family and friends were invited to visit, and I went to see him in his room. After he had updated me on all the new friends he'd made, I knew I had to tell him something. This was the reason for my visit.

"Stephen, I'm going to move out of the apartment for a while." I looked down at the table. This was so hard. Stephen looked deeply into my eyes and nodded, looking like he felt all the pain he had ever caused me. Finally I met his gaze. "I don't want a divorce. I just think we need some distance so you can work on your sobriety, and I can focus on me."

"I understand." He tried not to show any regret or sadness, but I could see his disappointment in himself.

There I was, separating from my husband while he was sick in rehab. It felt complicated, because one of the tenets of my sobriety is to forgive, to see people as sick and doing their best rather than as evil. But all that didn't change the fact that I did not trust Stephen. It didn't mean that I had to sit and take the abuse when he turned into a monster. True, he wasn't himself when he was using, but that didn't change the fact that he was dishonest and verbally abusive. I knew Stephen was a good man. But I also needed to be sure that the drugs were gone.

After his second rehab program ended, I moved into the small apartment in Venice under a three-month lease. Stephen moved back into our apartment and worked through the 12 Steps.

I kept working and stayed as busy as I could.

When Stephen got to Step Eight, making amends, it had turned to autumn. He flew to Chicago for a day to see my parents. He had the cab drop him off at a flower shop near my childhood home, where he picked up a bouquet for my mom and planned to walk the rest of the way. Then, just like in the movies, a clap of thunder rang out and it started raining.

"A sprinkle never hurt anyone."

With that cue, it started POURING. Stephen was instantly drenched, and the flowers looked like they'd gone ten rounds with a kangaroo. He knocked on my parents' door and my mother opened it, completely surprised to see a wet man in a drenched suit.

"Erm. Hello." Stephen waved awkwardly.

"I'll get you a towel." My mom rushed from the door, leaving Stephen to stand next to my dad uncomfortably.

My dad clapped him on the back. "Went for a swim, huh? Not very good weather for that. Weird decision to make."

"Do you mind if we all sit down together? I'd like to read something to you both."

My parents glanced at each other. My mom handed him the towel and led him to the living room couch.

Stephen pulled a soggy letter out from his pocket. He carefully peeled it open and drew a shaky breath, sitting on the long floral couch right where I used to watch infomercials every night as a child until I fell asleep. He read his amends to them.

My parents both stared at him. They weren't used to apologies or direct, earnest communication. Or people who were willing to change. My mom felt the urge to fill the silence. "Ummmm. That's really nice."

Stephen continued, "Please, I want to work to make this better."

"You're still wet, let me—let me get you a new towel." My mom rushed to the linen closet.

Abandoned, my dad tapped his heel awkwardly. Then he pointed to Stephen's arms. "You been going to the gym?"

My mother was aware of what had been going on. I had told her about the pills and how mean he had gotten. But my dad . . . it was all news to him, and deep emotional confrontations aren't really his forte.

"Um, not so much recently."

"You know, when I go to the gym I listen to an iPod. I play some Nirvana, a little Beatles . . . you know, the greats. That just makes the whole experience better. And then—wham bam—you've run a mile! Good stuff, those iPods." My dad then got up and joined my mother over near the towel closet.

Ultimately, they could really see the effort that Stephen was putting in. After all, he didn't just make a phone call to apologize. He flew all the way there, walked for miles in the rain, and flew back the next day. It was the perfect triumph of a great effort, bad planning, and some lousy luck.

In AA, they say that you have to be willing to go to any lengths to complete the steps. I could see that he was willing. I was living on my own in the Venice apartment when one day, I got a call from him.

"Hello, Laura."

"How's it going?"

He cleared his throat. "If you're free tonight, I'd like to—if you don't mind, I think it would be nice if—can I take you out on a date tonight?"

"Okay."

He took me out that night to this cute diner in between our houses.

We started to laugh again. At the end of the date, he took me straight home. A few days later:

"Can I take you out again tonight?"

"Café Gratitude?"

"Let's do it."

That night we arrived at the restaurant, and right as we got seated a chipper server came up to us. "Hi, my name's Jeffrey, and I'll be your server today. What makes you happy?"

Stephen and I looked at each other awkwardly. I forgot that the servers ask you a cheesy (but still vegan) question every time you eat there. I'm all for gratitude, but tonight I wasn't in the mood.

"Butts."

Stephen smiled at Jeffrey. "Yes. For me as well: butts."

We started over slowly. We dated again. Eventually, he asked me to move back in with him. Once I trusted him completely, I did.

I believe that people can change. If they have the willingness, if they see a need within themselves, they can reach down within and change. I hate when people use the phrase "you are who you are" as an excuse to let themselves be less than the person they could be. Stephen did a really thorough inventory on himself and made one of the most difficult changes possible. He hit bottom and got better because he wanted to live. I could see it in his actions and I could feel it.

Remember when I had my relapse at six months of sobriety? That was when I learned that I had to put my sobriety before everything else. That struggle gave me the courage to get my own place and have space from Stephen. It doesn't mean I didn't love him dearly through all of it. I never stopped loving him, but I knew that I had to put my sobriety first. I had to have faith that if we were meant to

209

be together, we would be. It was either trust the universe, or stay with Stephen and enable his addiction. If I had just been okay with everything he was doing, he would have just kept doing it. In the end, I believe it made him stronger and he is a better man than the one I met at that party. He's kinder, more compassionate, more loving. He truly appreciates every day that he is alive, and that's a wonderful way to live.

It was a bit past our second anniversary when we finally looked around our Santa Monica apartment and decided we couldn't be there anymore. The whole space was filled with bad memories. The fighting, the abuse, and the lies all took place here. We weren't in that place anymore mentally, so why should we be there physically? We decided to move out and start over, fresh.

We found a beautiful house in the Hollywood Hills, next to Frank Zappa's old house. Joni Mitchell was down the street. It had this sweet 1960s Laurel Canyon vibe. Our neighbor across the street was this seventy-five-year-old gay hippie who would always have these massive, crazy parties. Stephen and I had a window on the second story of our house that looked out onto the street . . . and honestly, sometimes it was better than watching TV. The neighbor would blast heavy metal in the morning and sometimes have busloads of little people trekking inside to his parties. We saw so many of his young boyfriends coming in and out of the house. It became our favorite thing to guess what the drama was between him and the twenty-five-year-old blond hottie, or if he was going to make it last with the thirty-year-old swoopy-haired one. It was the best when they would have actual yelling matches, so we could finally hear the dialogue.

"You have my cat, man! It's not your cat, give me back my cat!!" yelled the swoopy-haired guy from the front driveway.

"You're not getting the cat!" Our neighbor yelling from his house.

"Well I'm not leaving until you give me the cat!" Then he threw his bag down onto the ground.

Okay, so many questions. We really needed more on this couple. With both of us standing at our second-story window, I turned to Stephen: "Popcorn?"

"Oh, that would be good. I think we'll be here awhile. Don't you?"

I smiled. "I do."

CHAPTER 10

Maggie: Cat

The story of Maggie begins on my third date with Stephen. I casually mentioned to him how much I loved cats, because that is *textbook* how to get a guy. Stephen looked at me thoughtfully and said, "Then let's get one."

"Um. What?"

"Let's go rescue a cat. Why not?"

"You want to rescue a cat?"

"Come on, Laura. Let's go."

The next day we headed over to the animal shelter in Compton. There was this tiny gray cat in a cage, small as my palm. He was so friendly and loving, and he immediately got into my hand and started purring.

"Stephen, look at this one."

"Awwwww." Stephen came over and scratched the kitten's head. "I love him. Let's take him home."

"NOPE," a voice said.

We looked up to see a stressed-out-looking woman with her hands on her hips. "That one is part of a set. You take him, then you take his sister. The black-and-white one. No one is separating them."

"What black-and-white one?"

She pointed to the farthest corner of the cage. Half shrouded in darkness and half burrowed underneath cardboard shavings was a terrified-looking calico kitten. I tried to reach for her, but she didn't budge from her spot. Okay!

I turned to Stephen. "Well, I guess we need to get this one to get the gray one."

Stephen looked nervous. "Um. Two cats? How much would you be coming over to see them and pet them and such—"

"You know what," the lady continued, "those two came in twenty minutes ago. You don't even have to fill anything out. Just take them."

Oh my God, how easy! "We can just take them, Stephen!"

Stephen feigned enthusiasm pretty well. "I heard! How . . . brilliant."

I walked out of the animal shelter with one kitten in each palm. Later I found out that Stephen doesn't even like cats. He had one when he was little and it was an angry little fucker that would bite and scratch him all the time. So he was a little afraid of them. He just wanted me to come over all the time and he was willing to do anything to make that happen. Which is sweet, but also totally insane. Suddenly he was stuck with two of them running around his apartment, peeing on everything, and climbing into his guitar amp. He didn't even think about the fact that he would be stuck with these cats forever if our relationship didn't work out.

But, bygones, because we had them now! We named the gray one Allen after my grandfather. Totally kidding—that would actually make sense. Our actual nonsense reason was that naming a cat "Allen" just made us both laugh really hard.

The skittish black-and-white one, though, we did name after someone we knew. We decided to call her Maggie, after my childhood best friend (who, by the way, is still very much a part of my life). When I posted a picture of Maggie (the cat) on Instagram with her name as the caption, I got a text from Maggie (the human) that just said: "Really, Laura?"

Now, my conversations with Stephen about Maggie go like this:

"Oh God, Maggie is pissing everywhere again."

"Cat or human?"

"Cat, but perhaps human as well. I haven't checked in with her this week." It's a valid question, seeing how much Maggie and I peed in public as kids.

The way the cats were at the shelter pretty much stayed the same as their whole personalities developed. Allen was fearless, loving, and kind; and Maggie constantly thought she was going to get murdered. Maggie sort of has the traits of an untreated alcoholic. She'll steal Allen's food and eat all of it, but she never knows when enough is enough. And just like an alcoholic . . . Maggie eventually hit her rock bottom.

When Stephen and I moved from the one-bedroom apartment to the two-bedroom apartment in Santa Monica, the cats were so upset. Cats HATE moving. They hate moving more than they hate water. It just makes no sense to them. Why leave your home for a new home where you don't know where all the footholds are and you have to relearn how to climb into all the drawers? I actually agree with them: moving sucks.

Maggie was stalking around all wide eyed and scared. As soon as we got settled in, she made a break for it. I think she wanted to find the old apartment, her REAL home. Two days passed and I was so worried. She wasn't familiar with these streets. She didn't know how to come back. Stephen, on the other hand, was fully convinced that she was dead. "Well, the circle of life," he'd said with a shrug.

Allen would go out to look for her. He'd cry out here and there, but after a while he just accepted the reality that she was gone. Animals are great teachers in that way; they get on with life quickly.

I, however, was not ready to get on with my life. One week turned into two, two turned into three, and eventually she had been gone a whole month. Every day, I would go to our local animal rescue, asking if anyone had seen a skittish black-and-white cat.

"No, sorry."

And then again: "No, sorry."

And then: "No, Laura, sorry. We just got an orange one in though. His name is Hamilton. Want to take a look?"

The employee at the shelter, Craig, was a skinny boy who always wore the same baggy shelter-volunteer T-shirt. The next time I ran into the rescue, Craig was sweeping the floor. He looked up and automatically said, "She's not here, Laura."

"But did you look??"

"Yes. It's my job to look! I'm always looking! Laura, cats don't come back home after a month."

No! This wasn't true! Maggie was my freaked-out, skittish, black-and-white CHILD. She was *not* gone.

"*Your mom* doesn't come back home after a month!"

"What?"

"YOUR MOM—I don't know . . . I'm sorry."

Craig put a hand on my shoulder. "It's okay. Grief is difficult."

"Your mom's difficult," I whispered. But he heard me. And then demanded I get the fuck out of his shelter.

I wasn't about to give up hope, though. One night at around four a.m., I heard a cry from outside my window. It wasn't so much a cry as a horrified meow. I ran out onto the balcony and there she was, looking like she had just stepped off the battlefield. She had scaled up the wall to the second story of the building and climbed over our balcony. She was wheezing! CATS DON'T WHEEZE.

I hurriedly pulled her inside and took a look at her in the light. This black-and-white cat was now completely black. She was covered in dirt and so skinny. She was crying. I put a bowl of food in front of her and she dove into it, eating as fast as she could and crying at the same time. And then she would throw it all up. We've all been there, am I right? No? Anybody?

She repeated this for an intense ten minutes: eating, crying, throwing up, crying, eating again. It must have been a while since she had eaten, because her body just wouldn't accept food. When she was done, I placed her in the sink and washed her fur. On a normal day, she would have scratched my face off if I tried to bathe her, but Maggie was so dirty and exhausted that she just accepted it.

The next day we took her to the veterinarian (with a short pit stop at the shelter to prove to Craig that miracles *do* happen). The vet checked her out and found nothing wrong with her except a urinary tract infection. Really Maggie, a UTI? Must have been living it up in the great outdoors.

Since then, Maggie has never tried to get out again. She's got some heavy PTSD from whatever happened out there. It was like she went on this crazy month-long binge, hit rock bottom, and won't ever do it again. It's just incredible that she found her way back.

Maggie and Allen feel like my spiritual teachers sometimes. Allen goes through life leading with love, and Maggie leads with fear. I learned this from reading *A Return to Love* by Marianne Williamson, which says that we are constantly in a state of either love or fear, and these states control the choices we make and the way we live. This idea really helped me in early sobriety because I used to be so fear-driven. I was hindered by this self-seeking fear that I was going to lose what I had or not get what I wanted. Then I read this book and realized that I could choose to lead with love and walk through my fear. I chose to start looking at life through a loving, giving lens, asking every day what I could give rather than what I could get. I wanted to know what my life would look like if I focused on tolerance and forgiveness. The answers are right in front of me in the form of Maggie and Allen. I'd either be happily basking in the sun and getting belly rubs from everyone around me or vomiting and crying next to my food bowl at four in the morning.

Then there's our one-eyed pug, Oliver. I have to preface this with the fact that there is nothing spiritual about Oliver.

Three years after we got married, Stephen would hint that he wanted a dog by randomly texting me dog pictures. Some guys send dick pics, Stephen sends dog pics. That turned into full-on links to dog profiles on adoption websites. And that turned into pulling me into animal shelters to "just peruse."

Dogs are a huge responsibility that I didn't know if we were ready for. We already had Maggie and Allen, and although they were both very low-maintenance pets, another pet just felt like a lot. One morning we went out for coffee, and as we were walking back to the car, we saw a pug rescue nearby. Stephen's face lit up.

"Let's just look," he said while hopping around like a kid on sugar.

"If we go in, we're going to walk out of there with like ten pugs!"

"No, no, let's just look! I can just look!"

Yeah right, but I said okay and we walked inside. And then . . . I saw them. Just tons of ugly, misfit pugs. Pugs are pretty weird-looking to begin with, but since this was a rescue, these ones were next-level funky-looking. Which is to say they were amazing and I WANTED THEM ALL.

Stephen went off on his own with so much exuberance it was like his dreams were coming true. I strolled around and then saw him. The One.

He was facing a wall, not moving, except for some nervous twitching. I picked him up and he started foaming at the mouth. I think that means he likes me? He had only one eye, which hopefully explained the staring at the wall. He was super skinny. The dog slipped through my hands a little; he was . . . gooey. Did something spill on him? I took a closer look at his skin and saw that it was irritated, oozing pus and goo. He was fucking disgusting.

From across the room, I saw Stephen holding one pug in each hand.

"Laura, look at these!" He had a healthy-looking black one, replete with two eyes, and a cute beige one, also with two eyes.

"Look at *this* one!" I turned the gooey pug around to face Stephen.

"JESUS!" Stephen startled at the sight of him. He composed himself and asked, "Are you sure that is a dog?"

"He is more dog than you'll ever be," I lashed out. The dog's mouth foam dripped onto my hand.

"Well at least he's . . . alive, isn't he?"

"He's hanging on! Let's take him home."

Stephen's joy at getting a dog quickly surpassed his disgust at my choice of a gooey, one-eyed pug. We spoke to the employee about taking him home. She frowned. "I don't think you want that one. He can't, um . . . he can't see very well."

"Yes, we want him," I interjected before Stephen could express any doubts.

The employee picked up another dog. "Have you seen Kathy? Just take her for a spin. Kathy is just awesome. So smart, SO funny. She LOVES to watch TV. Her fav show is *Judge Judy*. Just don't even flip the channel while it's on or she'll bite your fucking face off."

I just wanted the goo dog. Who else was going to rescue the pug facing the wall? We signed the paperwork to take home our new dog. We named him Oliver.

We headed to his foster mom's house to go pick him up, and Oliver was itching his goo-skin like crazy. His foster mom was so friendly and clearly drunk, so when I asked her why he was itching so much, she said, "Oh, he's just crazy."

I looked down at Oliver, who was facing a wall again. "Can he see?"

She took another sip from her "coffee" mug. "Completely. That one eye really does the job. He's just crazy!"

We brought him home and put him in the living room, but he kept bumping into stuff. I looked at Stephen, worried. "I feel . . . like that eye doesn't work."

We took him to the vet to get his eyes checked out and learned that he was 100% blind. Also he's allergic to everything. Okay, that makes sense! We found out that in his last home, the owners kept him in a dark garage and neglected him. With so much time in the dark, he slowly lost his vision. After he became completely blind, he bumped into a sharp object that pierced his eye. The owners checked on him days later, after it had gotten infected and it was too late to save the eye.

Living with Oliver had really changed my perception of dogs. Now when I see a fully working, two-eyed dog that can do things like find his water bowl and not hit his head on everything, I'm just so impressed. *What else can you do, work the front desk at a gym?* All of the people who had come in contact with Oliver told us he would never do things like a normal dog. He would never be able to go on walks, or play fetch, or poop in the right spots.

I didn't want anyone to limit Oliver! This dog was going to learn to play fetch. I threw his favorite toy and he would sniff around the living room trying to find it. A minute passed . . . then five . . . then ten. By then I had forgotten we were playing and turned on the TV. And then . . . *squeak squeak*! He had found it! When Oliver successfully fetches his toy . . . it's like he's won the Olympics. It's like WE won the Olympics.

One day I was working upstairs and heard Oliver crying from the floor below. I came out to see him trapped on the first step of our staircase. He was too scared to go up, and too scared to jump down. I picked him up and brought him upstairs with me.

The next day I came out to the stairs to see Oliver on the third step, crying.

The next day he was on the FIFTH step before he started crying. Would our fantastic blind dog beat the odds and be able to climb a whole staircase?

The answer is yes. He did it once. And then he might have gotten overwhelmed when I screamed for ten minutes, "WHO'S A GOOD

BOY?" After that, he never tried again, but who needs mobility when you can just get airlifted up the stairs by humans?

Oliver is a real rags-to-riches story. He was a rescue, and now he has forty-thousand followers on Instagram telling him what a good boy he is every minute of every day.

I don't know if he can hear me anymore. We used to clap and then he could find us, but now he doesn't really respond to sounds.

That's okay. He still has normal dog experiences like going for walks (we carry him around in a bag because he is too scared to walk) and visiting dog parks (he sits in the center of the field feeling overwhelmed and foaming at the mouth) and playing with Allen and Maggie (Maggie hides from him and Allen boxes him in the face and Oliver gets scared because he can't see where the blows are coming from).

If I was still drinking and using, I would never have thought to rescue an animal. I never wanted to take care of any being other than myself. It was always me first—I needed to be able to do what I wanted when I wanted to. The biggest part of my sobriety was changing from self-seeking to being of service to others. "Others" includes carrying my very special Oliver to his water bowl as often as he needs. I've gotten to experience so much joy living with these animals. They're my goofy-looking family of misfits, and I wouldn't change them for the world.

Sometimes I look at them and I feel so lucky. I'm lucky I found Stephen. I'm lucky he spontaneously agreed to cats. I'm lucky Oliver isn't gooey anymore and I can take good care of him and all his needs. All of these things feel like the gifts of sobriety to me; reminders of why I'm so happy to be who I've become.

CHAPTER 11

Walking Through Fear

I'm a completely rational person. Well, okay, I am NOW. But . . . certain things just get to me. Before I started creating my own content, I was a working actor, supporting myself solely by booking jobs. I didn't give myself a plan B, and that worked. But . . . I wasn't where I wanted to be. I was auditioning all the time, I'd book a pilot and it wouldn't get picked up, I'd get a call back and then they'd offer the role to someone else. It was this constant anxiety and stress and lack of control over my career.

When I booked a role, I'd feel this urge for a more interesting character to dig into. I'd been acting so long, every character felt like repetition. I wanted better lines and more complexity, but you know what? Who cares! Give me another airhead model to play because THAT'S APPARENTLY ALL I CAN DO.

See? The grind was getting to me.

I wanted so badly to be on the next *Friends*, to be the next Lisa

223

Kudrow. I got so angry I wasn't on a sitcom that I did not want sitcoms on in the house.

Stephen loves sitcoms though. So . . . he had to watch them secretly in the bathroom. My eyes would narrow if I were getting dressed in the bedroom and could hear the faint sounds of . . . "IS THAT A LAUGH TRACK?"

"What? No! It's just fetish porn!"

I'd burst into the bathroom and snatch the iPad from his hands. "*The IT Crowd*, Stephen?!"

"I'm so sorry. Chris O'Dowd just gets me."

I was SO angry I wasn't on a show like that, that I had to GO FOR A TWENTY-TWO-MINUTE WALK.

After one of these meltdowns, Stephen came home with a camera. He handed it to me. "You have characters. You can write. Create your own stuff. Post videos on YouTube. Think of your own series and shoot it."

Stephen was so supportive of me. That, or he wanted to watch his sitcoms in peace. Either way, he was one of the first people in my ear saying, "You can do this." He was a huge inspiration for me. But also, no. How could I post videos of myself online? That was terrifying. And it didn't seem like a "real" path to my goals. How was making videos going to get me on the next *Friends*?

I was so tired of the audition grind, and I had been for a long time. Years earlier, I decided to try stand-up. I knew I wanted to write and be a creator, and stand-up was the only way I knew of doing this. I was around twenty years old and I was a total noob. I had no idea which open mic to go to, so I hopped on the computer and googled BEST COMEDY OPEN MIC.

The first result was for The Comedy Store on Sunset. That sounds good, right? Little did I know that The Comedy Store is NOT where first-time stand-ups go. It's where already-famous stand-ups go to surprise their fans. It's where veterans go to try out their new material. It's not—I repeat—NOT a gentle crowd. New comedians are supposed to go deep into the Valley to Joe's Café and Check-Cashing Open Mic or something like that. But nope, twenty-year-old, never-done-stand-up-before Laura Clery went to The Comedy Store. To make matters worse, I had no idea what my comedic voice was at the time. I tried really hard to fit into what I thought female comedians had to be—basically Janeane Garofalo. I wore thick-rimmed glasses and spoke in a really monotone, deadpan voice. It was so not me: I was blonde and overly animated.

I got up on the stage and looked out at the faces in the audience. They were looking for any reason in the world not to laugh. My sister Colleen and her friend Rebecca were the only smiling faces. I cleared my throat awkwardly and told a very stupid story.

"How many people here hate getting haircuts? Show of hands. No one? One person right there, great."

I tried to be very cool, but I was very not cool. I got through the set as fast as I could. To say I bombed would be an understatement. It was Pearl Harbor. I finished my set to a few halfhearted cheers from Colleen and Rebecca and I skulked off the stage in shame. The emcee came onstage after me, took the mic, and pointed to me.

"That was Laura Clery! Looks she's a ten, comedy she's a two!"

Colleen and Rebecca were cringing so hard in the audience. We all ditched the rest of the show. I don't remember the rest of that night because I went home and drank it all away. I was so scarred from that experience that I didn't try stand-up again for years.

But four years later, I was very sober and desperately needing a

LAURA CLERY

creative outlet. Too sober, one could say! I was pacing my apartment anxiously. I left and came back with a bottle of vodka. I stared at it. Either I go to an open mic, or I drink. I stared at the bottle. I was so scared to try comedy again, but the alternative was staring me in the face. I do my art or I drink.

I opened the bottle and smelled it, the harsh smell that brought with it flashes of bad memories from nights that I blacked out. I poured it down the drain, grabbed my keys, and left.

I drove deep into the valley to a random bar. I walked inside. This bar was the definition of depressing. It was western-themed, complete with bartenders in cowboy hats. I asked for a cup of water. There were four people in the audience—all of them were sad, struggling comedians waiting for their turn on the mic. None of them laughed at the guy telling jokes onstage. The better his joke, the less the audience wanted to give him the laughs. It was kind of awful.

When it was finally my turn, I walked up onstage, thankfully without the thick-rimmed glasses and monotone voice. I just told the story of my sandwich phase. You know, the phase we all go through where we get obsessed with buying homeless people sandwiches? No? Just me? Okay. When I was getting sober, it became part of my daily routine. Every day around noon, I'd find a new homeless person near my local Subway and say "Hey, can I get you a sandwich?" It wasn't normal. I did it so often that the employees would wince every time they saw me come in.

There was one especially shy homeless guy who I had to coax into the store. I asked him if I could get him a five-dollar foot-long and he was like, "No . . . no, it's okay."

"Come on, seriously, it's fine."

"I'm not hungry."

"Your sign literally says that you're hungry. What can I get you?"

"Okay fine. Just a chicken sandwich."

I walked inside, ordered, and got out my wallet to pay. The employee looked at me. "Anything else?"

The homeless guy stepped closer. "Actually yeah, can I get extra chicken, extra tomatoes, extra spinach, a side of bacon, and can you put chips on it?"

Cool, I guess he had finally come out of his shell. Now the five-dollar foot-long came to fourteen dollars.

Up onstage, I finished my story and heard laughter ring out. Holy fuck! I did WELL. For the first time! And the sweetest part was that I was just being me. I was telling the most-me story I had. One of the other comics came up afterward and said, "If you keep going, you're going to be huge. You've got it."

Holy shit, I can do this! I started doing open mics all the time. I was newly sober and just fucking doing it. I wasn't letting fear run my life anymore. I became part of this total grind of going to bars late at night, staying until like two a.m. and performing for six other bitter comedians, honing our craft together and working our asses off. After about four months of stand-up, my agent got me a spot at The Comedy Store on a show with Natasha Leggero and some other really funny comics. Holy fuck, there I was in the place that first tore me down. But I was a lot stronger now. My sponsor came to this one. It was amazing. I did a five-minute set about this yoga instructor I had once, who called everything delicious. She even referred to her friend's baby as "delicious." It was weird. As I told the joke onstage, I became her as a character. I was integrating my strengths: storytelling, characters, and comedy. It worked! Someone from the TV show *The League* was in the audience that night, saw my character, and realized I would be great for the part of a yoga instructor on their show. They straight-up offered me the role that night. It was incredible.

But stand-up wasn't exactly the right fit for me. It felt . . . lonely. To make matters worse, it was really difficult for me to be around all the alcohol. I had to put my sobriety first. No matter how much I liked getting laughs, stand-up wasn't for me. There had to be another way.

Also . . . the grind takes years and it turns out, I'm not very patient. I typed into my Facebook status: *There has to be a way I can reach MORE people more quickly!*

One day, I was on my way home from a pilot audition and I got the call to let me know that they offered the role to Mandy Moore. Like, good for Mandy Moore. But also, why even bring me in and waste my time? I was so done with this shit. I didn't want to be strung along. I didn't want to be a random face they brought in to an audition to prove to Mandy Moore that this role was in high demand. I was done.

But what else could I do? I racked my brain while I walked. I remembered this girl, Porsche, who I met at a Capital One commercial. She had hit me up afterward, asking if I wanted to make something with her. I had brushed it off, not really knowing what a web series even entailed. But you know what? I wanted to create and make my own destiny.

I called her. "Hey Porsche. I'm in."

"Hey Laura. In what?"

"Oh sorry, in the web series thing."

"Oh right! Cool babe, let's do it."

Porsche is a beautiful, stunning black model who I met on a shoot where neither of us had lines. We both played runway models. I didn't know how well we worked together or whether she was a good writer or even a sane person! I did know that I didn't want to audition anymore—I wanted to create.

I smiled. "Fuck yeah. Come over tomorrow and we'll write it."

The next day she came over to our apartment.

"I had this idea to write a web series about how absurd the modeling industry is. Laura, it's so funny."

Ideas just started flowing. Without moving from the couch, we wrote a pilot that day. We came up with this series called *Hungry* about two aging, struggling models who were incredibly underqualified to do anything else. They were figuratively and literally hungry. It was the first script I finished since getting sober, and it felt so good. We pitched the show to Russell Simmons's production company, All Def Digital, and they greenlit it. They loved it!

Russell gave us our first show. I wrote, produced, and starred in the whole first season alongside Porsche. All of a sudden I was on the other side of the casting table. I was auditioning people, and I LIKED it. This was where I wanted to be, dude. I get to create the characters and write and act? I'm never doing that other bullshit again. I felt like a fish in water. We got King Bach to direct. At the time, he was this up-and-coming YouTuber with fifty thousand followers! (Now he has like twenty million.) After it was posted, we had an automatic reach to All Def's one-hundred-thousand subscribers.

It was my first taste of making something and having it SEEN.

It was weird. I went from network TV to YouTube. It wasn't glamorous and the money definitely wasn't there, but I didn't care. I was finally doing what I wanted to be doing. To make things better, it was received well. Before, I had wanted more than anything to be on the next *Friends*, but now . . . I was doing YouTube. And I felt so fulfilled.

My goals had shifted. I didn't feel the need to be on a sitcom anymore. I just wanted to make as many people laugh as possible. THAT was my goal. I wanted to be creative and have my creativity bring other people joy.

I pulled out my laptop and the camera that Stephen bought me. My next project would be called "Product of a Sperm Donor." The premise was this: A man had donated his sperm 173 times and he had 173 children all over the world. I wanted to interview them all. Each video was going to be an interview between me and one of the half siblings.

First of all, why 173? I chose a really high goal for my first project. It should have been thirty, tops. I think I made twelve and then I was like . . . okay, that's enough. The twelve interviews were cool, though. Since they were half siblings, they could all look similar and I could play them all. But they could also be from different countries and I could try out a wide range of characters.

It was the first thing I ever posted online. And no one watched it. I think the one comment was from my mom: "Great job, honey!"

I kept posting videos . . . and then deleting them. I was afraid of putting myself out there. Sure I had acted a thousand times on TV and in commercials and I had done *Hungry*, which was seen by a hundred thousand people, but all of those things were under other people's names. I had never spoken for myself before. I had never built my own brand. What if people hated it?

That morning I called my sponsor, Kristal.

"I'm really scared. I'm scared to build my own brand. What if people hate me? What if they hate what I have to say? Or worse, what if they don't care?"

Kristal sighed. "Laura. You're an artist. You make art. Stay in the action and out of the results."

It just clicked for me when she said that. I needed to do what I believed to be my purpose on this earth. I needed to create. It wasn't about the results. It was about the action!

I called my agents and told them to stop sending me out on auditions. I was done. They had been sending me out all the time for pilots, movies, and guest spots. It was taking too much energy from me, and 90% of the time I wouldn't get anything. Why not take all that time and create content my own way? From there, I just shot and shot and shot. I kept posting new characters and new ideas. Who cared if no one was watching? I was walking through my fear—this fear that I carried with me for my entire life. Stephen started to get involved too. He was scoring *Transformers* AND my Instagram videos. I would ask him to be in my videos and he would. He was so supportive. He would get into character without fear and took direction so well. We would just shoot and laugh. I posted a video a day for a year. I was throwing everything at the wall and seeing what stuck.

This was the time when Vine and fifteen-second Instagram videos were the language of the internet. I kept posting and posting to build that muscle and figure out what people wanted to see and what worked. I just had an idea and posted it. I was obsessed, but thankfully at the time, Stephen's career was taking off as well. He was making enough money that I could create without worrying about the next bill. I was so grateful for this freedom.

As I stopped worrying and started putting my true self

online . . . people started to take notice, and my following grew a bit. Having a small following is like having a few trading cards in your pocket. I started to put myself around other content creators and collaborate with them. We would feature each other's work or shoot with each other to expand our followings and get our names out there.

I noticed that all the creators at All Def were collabing with each other, so I inserted myself among them. It was so fun. Every day was just shooting videos and hanging out.

"I'll shoot your video if you shoot mine!"

"I'll shout you out if you shout me out."

The best part of creating videos and film in general is that you truly can't do it alone. You need other people to act and populate the world you're creating. At the very least, you need someone to hold the camera and press record for you. Collabing helped us all build our followings.

At the end of my year of posting one video a day, things slowed down a little for me. My following stayed consistent, but it wasn't growing anymore. Collabing started to be less effective because all the creators I knew were already in the same circles, sharing the same following.

Something needed to change. For some reason, I felt like the change had to come from within me.

I grew up with the mindset that there was never enough, life was hard, and you took what you could get. That mindset stayed with me, and I had been so negatively focused for a long time. I constantly thought about losing what I had. *What if*s filled my mind. *What if I lost my job? What if no one watched this video? What if I wasn't funny?* I'd had positive goals in the past, but they were so mundane:

I hope that I can make rent this month. I hope that I can book at least a commercial this week. Whatever I focused on I could achieve, but I was consistently focusing on the bare minimum I needed to survive. What if I thought bigger?

I started getting into the Law of Attraction. All the aspects of the Law of Attraction are pretty far out there, but what I took from it is this: rather than focusing on what you don't want, focus on what you do want. Don't be afraid to dream as big as you want. What you are thinking, what you tell yourself, can manifest. The concept was so mind-blowing to me, I started saying affirmations to myself every morning:

I am going to make millions of people laugh around the world on a consistent basis. I am going to have a successful career.

Then I took it further. I wasn't "going" to have these things. I wanted them to exist in the present:

I am so happy and grateful that I am making millions of people laugh with my videos.

I tried to shift my perception of myself as well:

I am smart. I am perfect as I am. I am enough. I am worthy.

It sounds cheesy, I know, but I had to do it. I had been depressed and thinking negatively of myself for as long as I could remember. Before this, I was writing in my journal, "I'm nothing. I should die. I don't deserve to live." These were the things that I thought about myself enough to actually write them down repeatedly in the yellow spiral notebook. Why the hell was I putting energy into that? Before I didn't know how to stop, but now I had figured it out. I spoke to myself every day to retrain my brain:

I am no better and no worse than anyone else. I am worthy. I am happy.

With a new sense of self underway, I honed in on my goal. I

wanted to make millions of people laugh all around the world. That was my new affirmation:

I'm making millions of people laugh all around the world.

I would picture people from all over the world watching my videos and laughing and feeling good because of something I did. It started to change the way I looked at my purpose, because I could give something to people. They might be anxious or depressed, and I could give them some goofy videos and make them laugh for a minute. For that one minute, they could forget their problems. I think that is amazing!

My affirmation was the first thing I would say in the morning, every single day. On the tenth day of saying that . . . I had my first viral video. The view count went up and up and up . . . until it was getting millions of views . . . being shared all over the world! I was literally making millions of people laugh all around the world. The video was of my Ivy character speaking to the camera in a breathy voice:

"Hey guys, it's me. Just wanted to remind you to never give up on your dreams. Like even if you want to. Just don't."

I thought it was so funny to have this out-of-touch character be the one trying to motivate people. The only problem was that in my affirmation, I didn't specify that the world would know who I was. The video was disconnected from me, reposted, and shared by millions of people who thought this character was a real person. I was honored! My performance was believable!

One morning I sprang out of bed with an idea. I nudged Stephen awake.

"Stephen. I have an idea. Will you film me cooking breakfast?"

Stephen was barely awake. "Who? What?"

I stared down at him intensely, amped up on ideas. "If I throw toast at you, just keep filming, okay?"

Stephen rubbed his eyes and rolled out of bed. "All right."

We walked into the kitchen and I did this repressed Southern housewife character who has a cooking show but can't stand her husband who's filming it. She's trying to teach the audience how to cook avocado toast, and meanwhile is bordering on killing her husband. This was the birth of my Pamela Pumpkin character. I showed it to a big YouTube-based production company and they picked it up as a series. I got to write, produce, and act in my second show. It was an incredible time of creative growth. I was trusting my intuition and shooting whatever I could think of. Four years earlier, this idea would have just died a lonely death in one of my journals next to the words: "I'm a piece of shit."

Now I was no longer afraid to fail. I realized that people liked what I had to offer and I wasn't delusional. I had something to give and I wanted to keep giving.

It was incredible to look out and see what I had accomplished. When I was doing stand-up open mics, I was reaching six people every time I performed. With digital content, I could reach hundreds of thousands of people, and I didn't even have to put on pants! If I framed the shot right, I didn't have to wear clothes at all! I didn't have to stay up until two a.m. every night at bars across Los Angeles; I didn't have to be around tons of drunk people and alcohol and drugs.

If stand-up had been the only way to be a creator, if there were no social media or online video sharing, I would have stuck with it. But I found this softer way to do what I love, which I happen to be good at. It just makes sense. This is right for me.

I kept growing, and I got a DM from the head of Kevin Hart's production company.

"Kevin Hart's a big fan. He wants you to create content for him."

Um, what? Kevin Hart knows who I am?

"Come in for a meeting!"

Um, WHAT? Okay! A few days later I went to his production company and Kevin Hart was standing there. "You're hilarious. I love your work. I'm creating a comedy app and I want you to create sketches for me."

Screams into the abyss

UM WHAAAAATTTTTT—

I wrote, directed, produced, and starred in thirty sketches for him. It wasn't much money, but it didn't matter. It was Kevin-fucking-Hart. He was a fan of mine? It gave me so much confidence.

After that, opportunities started knocking at my door. Brands were asking me to promote their products, and I finally started making steady money from my art. I would get new opportunities here and there. I finally knew who I was and I was solid. I had fully transitioned from actor to content creator.

It really sounds cheesy but those affirmations are what lifted me over the edge. I swear by them. I had such a rigid self-image before, and the only things that could break the cycle of self-hate were intentional, affirming statements. I've been depressed, anxious, and suicidal for much of my life, and this is what has turned it around for me. My brain has said so many mean things to me. I never want my brain to talk to me in THAT TONE AGAIN. *You hear me, Brain?*

What I imagined for myself could manifest in my world. So I started visualizing more:

A house in the hills with a pool. A house in the hills with a pool.

Then Stephen and I found the perfect one right when we had saved up enough money to move in. Growing up with no money had given me negative associations about money and people with money. I used to think people with money were greedy or selfish, but that's not necessarily true at all. I had to redefine the way I looked at wealth. The more you have, the more you can give. If you have a little bit of money you can give to homeless people on the street, but if you have a lot of money? There's a world of help you could give to others. I had to tell myself that it's okay to have money. It's okay not to struggle and suffer. It sounds so strange, but getting out of that survival mindset was so difficult. Now that I'm financially stable and saving up . . . my affirmations are getting even bigger.

My most recent philanthropic goal is to open an animal sanctuary. Animal rights are very important to me, so I started visualizing a sanctuary where we can rescue tons of animals from being put down. I was obsessing over it, and then I got a call from Colleen. "Laura, we went vegan and we have an eight-acre farm that we don't know what to do with."

"HELLO, SISTER. I HAVE AN IDEA."

I told her about my idea and she was very into it. Things are happening, people! The dots are connecting themselves.

I started to get even more specific with my affirmations. I'm making millions of people laugh around the world AND I have millions of followers. I was getting a ton of views and shares, but my follower count wasn't in the millions yet.

It's strange, people always ask how I got to where I am now, but there are truly no logical step-by-step instructions to get here. The internet is the Wild West, and I ended up with the perfect storm of willpower, talent, opportunity, and strange coincidence. The only thing I can recommend is to visualize. For the record, I am not saying this is magic. I'm saying that a shift in your focus from what you don't want to what you do want is more powerful than we could ever imagine, and it works in mysterious ways. There was no aspect of this success I could have truly planned for.

Similarly, I couldn't have planned that one day I would be sitting with Stephen and playing around on Snapchat, and then happen across this square-face filter. I literally laughed when I saw myself, turned to Stephen and said, "I think my battery is dead. Can I use your dick?"

"AW SICK, Laura! That's sick!" I couldn't have planned him being genuinely appalled in the most hilarious way. I kept doing these pickup lines, and his reactions were killing me every time. I just wanted to say the worst thing possible to make him cringe more and more. I wasn't even going to post this, it was just for me. But then I figured . . . why the fuck not?

I posted it and people started losing their shit. I thought, *Wow, I might be onto something here*. That was the video that really blew me up—now I finally had the millions of followers on Instagram and Facebook that I had been visualizing. More and more brands started contacting me, asking me to promote them. I started getting recognized on the street, which was so amazing and always unexpected. When I went to London, a woman yelled "I'M YOUR GREATEST SWEDISH FAN!!"

Whoa. I didn't know people even watched me over there!

I kept saying gross things to Stephen with the square-face filter and that entire series went viral. I have my theories about why this particular series stuck. There's so much comedy where the joke is that a dude is objectifying or sexually harassing a woman. To see a strong sexual woman dominating a guy and making him the sexual object . . . that's new. To me, this character is really for women. A lot of guys love her, too, but women *really* had this craving to see a female sexual pervert instead of the usual gross man over and over again. She's just trying to get some D! I think that just resonated with people, to the point where one British guy even has a tattoo of her on his arm!

I see so many content creators that create a video that really hits, really goes viral, and then . . . they immediately move on to the next thing. You see viral videos come and go all the time. So how does one take that and build a brand? The first thing I did was ask my followers to name her in a Facebook Live. I went live and ten minutes later my character was named Helen Horbath, which I thought was hilarious. She definitely looks like a Helen. (Sorry to everybody named Helen!)

After that, I thought about who Helen was as a person. Who was this square-faced sexual pervert? What is her mother like? Why the hell is she like this? I built out her entire world, her family, her home. And I shot it, calling it: *Me When I Visit Family*. I'm finally at the point where I have my own sitcom of Helen and her family on Facebook. That's how I evolved her from just a funny idea to an entire series with more than forty episodes so far. Once I let go of my goal of being on a sitcom and changed it to being of service—to spreading laughter—here I was, writing, directing, and starring in my own sitcom. It's one of the biggest show pages on Facebook, with more than five million fans who tune in every week to see Helen and her dysfunctional family.

Being a social-media influencer is not like anything else. I have direct communication with my fans. Immediately after I post some-thing, they will tell me if they like it or if they don't. I love being so close to them and talking to them and connecting to them. I once got a message from a man who said that he was going to kill himself that night, but he decided to scroll through Facebook first. He came across my videos and then started binging them . . . and that it was morning now and he was still alive. Messages like that are why I do what I do, but it does get overwhelming sometimes. I feel the pressure of wanting to make all these people happy. I want to please everyone and help everyone. I want to deliver the funniest content day after day and for people to love it. Chris Rock said that if you're going to listen to the fan who says you're a genius, you also need to listen to the fan who says you're a piece of shit. In the end, I have Kristal's wise words to bring me back to earth: stay in the action and out of the results.

—

Sometimes I think about Stevie Ryan, the girl who I did the *Sex Ed* pilot with—the first content creator/YouTuber I ever met. I looked up to her so heavily when I met her. She was really a model for me. She was an unapologetic woman who was smart and hilarious and unabashedly herself. She was making content when it wasn't cool; she was on YouTube when it was really the Wild West. I remember thinking I wanted to be just like her.

After she got really popular, she got her own show on VH1. She was entering the industry from the top and I thought that was amazing. Her show was this hilarious comedy sketch show where she played every character, but then it got canceled after two seasons.

After it got canceled . . . she sort of stopped creating content. She stopped doing what she loved, and in July 2017, she killed herself. At thirty-three years old, she hung herself in her apartment.

Her death affected me so deeply, because I saw so much of myself in her. We followed each other, and two months before she died, she hit me up.

"Let's shoot, dude!"

"Hell yes, let's shoot."

I really wanted to. The problem was, she was high all the time. Her Instagram was full of pictures of weed. No shade to her lifestyle, but it was really difficult for me to be around. She would wake up and get high and go to sleep high. It was all day every day for her, and that type of energy brought me too far back into my past. I couldn't do it.

A year before she died, I went to meet with a production company. They wanted to develop a show with me and Stevie. Honestly, it would have been perfect. Stevie and I were a perfect fit for each other. But I had to tell them no, even though I fucking loved her. It was because I knew that doing a TV show with someone meant being around them all day every day for months and months. I knew I couldn't be around someone whose life was dictated by getting high, someone who had to self-medicate so much. It was dangerous for me. I had to put my sobriety first and say no.

I just wish I had told her that there is a way out. I wish I had that chance to show her that she could get out of the hole she was stuck in. I knew where she was; I knew she was stuck in her addiction. All she had was her following and her art to keep her afloat, and when she stopped posting . . . that was it.

I can't speak for her, and I could be completely off base, but this

LAURA CLERY

is what I took from that situation: if I don't have that self-worth inside me, I won't survive the day that the likes stop coming and followers stop caring.

If you don't have this strong sense that you're enough regardless of the external situation, then content creation is such a dangerous business to be in. One day you're popular with strangers, and the next day you're nothing to them. If you define yourself by how others see you, then suddenly you're nothing to even yourself.

It's so strange to see someone's social media still up after their death. One of Stevie's last posts is a photo of her dousing herself in water with the caption: "Too hot out here for a coldhearted bitch like me." On brand 'til the end.

I'm a part of something so new and unregulated. I feel like there's this new addiction to likes and views and followers that drives a lot of creators out of control. It's proven that likes give our brains a hit of dopamine, so it makes sense the crazy lengths that creators will go to stay relevant. Why did Logan Paul film a dead guy? Because he would go to any length to get the views. That's his hit, his high, his self-worth. I think Logan chose the hit over considering what would be the compassionate thing to do. When you're an addict, nothing comes before that hit. Like when a meth-head is willing to steal all the stuff out of your suitcase to be able to sell it and get more meth.

I feel incredibly grateful that my success happened after I was solid in my sobriety. AA gave me the tools not only to handle my life without alcohol, but also to handle pressure. I was where Stevie was once. I barely held on, and I certainly didn't know why. When I finally got sober, I realized it was because I had a mission to make millions of people laugh. That's what I was put on this earth to do. I had a purpose that was more than drinking and using.

242

Every morning I do Tony Robbins's *Hour of Power*. It's cheesy as shit and I love it. It's how I use my morning wisely. If I get on my phone right when I wake up, then I become riddled with anxiety. The *Hour of Power* means that I open my eyes, put on my gym shoes, and get my endorphins going. Stephen and I walk a mile and a half down the hill from our house and back again. Yes, I power walk in the suburbs every morning just like your mom.

For the first fifteen minutes of the walk, I do breathing exercises to get centered. For the second fifteen minutes, I make a list of everything I'm grateful for. Stephen and I usually alternate. I say "I'm grateful I'm sober today," and he says "I'm grateful for our one-eyed dog," and so on. It puts us in a state of gratitude, which is a really easy way to make yourself feel good, even if you're in a bad mood. Then after that, we do fifteen minutes of visualization, where we list all the goals and hopes we have for ourselves as if they are already happening for us. "I'm so happy and grateful that we have an animal sanctuary." Then the final ten minutes is visualizing what you want to accomplish for the day as if it's already happened. "I'm so grateful that I finish shooting two videos and I start a script for tomorrow."

That's my morning. As Tony Robbins recommends, if you don't have an hour of power, then have thirty minutes to thrive or fifteen minutes to fulfillment or two minutes to tango. Two minutes is surely better than none. Every morning this hour leads me to start my day with a mindset of abundance. Abundance of friendship, love, and laughter. If you feel like you have it, then it will come.

Before I became who I am today, I shot a short film about all of this. I had this idea called *The Procrastinator*, where I played every character. Procrastination was like . . . my best quality. I was really great at it. You want me to reply to an email? Give me a month! You want a script written? Well, how about I say I will and then I don't! And then I'll never talk to you again because I feel guilty!

The film was about a girl who needed to mail a letter but kept getting distracted. It was as random as my brain. I hired a guy named Scott from ProductionHUB to shoot it, found this fifty-year-old guy named Earl (who really wanted to go to Wendy's for some reason) to do sound, and then Stephen produced and did everything else. The four of us were the entire crew.

The film opens with me waking up, grabbing a letter, and placing a stamp on it. As I head to the mailbox I run into my old Russian landlady (me in a fat suit), who stops me and berates me.

"You have to pay rent! You are late!"

I fight with her for a while and then turn down an alley where I find this homeless crackhead (me with my teeth blacked out) who asks for any food I might have. I give her my bag of almonds and she throws them on the ground and stomps on them.

"Hey, why are you stomping on those??"

"I ain't got no teeth!" (She was pureeing them.)

Then I keep walking to the mailbox, but I stop inside a nail salon and get my nails done by a hysterical woman (me with makeup running down my face). Then we did a whole musical number at the nail salon, and the nail salon woman turns out to be magical. Because of course she was. I felt around in my pockets . . . and I had dropped the piece of mail. I went back home a failure. Or! A very successful procrastinator.

As I got in the house, Stephen walked by in a carrot costume, holding a briefcase and saying, "I'm off to work!" It was all very *cinema verité*.

Then, the crackhead found the letter and brought it back to my house. We had dinner together—pureed dinner, of course. All's well that ends well! Except the letter never got sent.

That film was completely emblematic of who I used to be. I've had so many distractions throughout my life, so many things getting in the way of my goals. I knew I would get to LA, I knew I would be acting, but the path here has been a winding road, full of dead-ends, U-turns, and random trips to Mexico. Somehow, I've ended up in an incredible industry that didn't exist when I was first dreaming about my future. How did I ditch all the distractions and get here? I saw that my addiction, my fear, and my insecurity were getting in the way of my purpose and I changed, even when I thought change was impossible. Today, I know people can change. I went from being a selfish, suicidal, self-obsessed, drug-addicted alcoholic, to being a more-happy-than-not, vegan, sober yogi with three rescue pets, making an effort to give back every day. In no way am I suggesting that it is easy or simple or magic. My change took years of effort and tons of mistakes and a few near-death experiences.

I get to do what I love every day. I get to make millions of people laugh around the world, and I get to be of service in that way. And it is because I put down drugs and alcohol and started walking through fear and wanting to be loving and tolerant and forgiving and of service. I decided that I want to be a good person. I think that works. I love my family, my career, and everyone reading this. Yes, you! Hey. Look at me. I love you! Now kiss me. Ohhhh yeah, that feels good. Mmmmm . . . Kiss me again. Okay, I'll stop making it weird. I clearly do not know how to end a book.

Oh and by the way, Stephen and I just had a baby. But that's another book. . . .

Acknowledgments

First of all, I need to thank Stephen Hilton, my incredible husband. You bought me a camera when I was broke and encouraged (forced) me to shoot out my ideas. You laughed at my jokes when no one else did. Thank you. I love you more today.

To my son, Alfie, you are perfect. Even though you unapologetically pee on me three times a day. You were born shortly after this book was finished or believe me, there would be several chapters describing your impossibly chubby cheeks. I love you.

To my loving and ever-so-tolerant family. Thank you for not murdering me. Mom, you have always been there for me, no matter what. (She's literally soothing Alfie to sleep right now as I attempt to finish this book.) Dad, you taught me to think for myself. I've always admired you. Tracy, you helped me graduate high school and bought me new jeans just because. And Colleen, you saved my life. Many times.

Thank you to my DG-to-LA besties, Jack, Holly, Maggie, and

Jill, for always showing up. Our friendship has kept me (somewhat) sane. Till death do us part, bishes.

Thank you to Alyssa Lerner for lovingly listening to my more-often-than-not humiliating tale with never any judgment. You are so so talented and without you this book would not have been complete . . . ted . . . until 2060.

To my incredibly kind hearted manager, Larry Shapiro, for endlessly encouraging me to walk through fear. Thank you for sticking with me. And for not being a douchebag.

Thank you to Gallery Books, Simon & Schuster, and my brutally honest editor, Jeremie Ruby-Strauss, for never hesitating to tell me "This sucks." You make good books great. Also big thanks to Brita Lundberg, Carolyn Reidy, Jon Karp, Jen Bergstrom, Aimèe Bell, Jen Long, Jen Robinson, Rachel Brenner, Abby Zidle, Tara Schlesinger, Mackenzie Hickey, Anabel Jimenez, Lisa Litwack, John Vairo, Alexis Minieri, Caroline Pallotta, Allison Green, Rosa Burgos, Chelsea Cohen, and Mike Kwan for all of your hard work. And to Elisa Rivlin, who waited nervously through every contraction. (I was in early labor during our last phone call. True story.)

Last but certainly not least, THANK YOU to my fans. Without you I would definitely be homeless. I have no other skill set. (And I'm fine with that.)